Marketing Your Creative Portfolio

animators
architects
artists
fine crafters
desktop publishers
fashion designers
graphic designers
illustrators
industrial designers
interior designers
jewelers
landscape designers
new media designers
photographers
product designers
among others

A workbook for
visual/spatial learners

by **Buff Hungerland**
Illustrations by
Tom Troisch

Marketing Your Creative Portfolio

Making the Leap from Creating a Portfolio to Getting a Job as a Professional Creative

Upper Saddle River, NJ 07458

Library of Congress Cataloging-in-Publication Data

Hungerland, Buff.
  Marketing your creative portfolio : making the leap from creating a portfolio to getting
a job as a professional creative / by Buff Hungerland ; illustrated by Tom Troisch.
    p. cm.
  ISBN 0-13-097733-0
  1. Art portfolios. 2. Artists—Vocational guidance. I. Title.

  N8350 .H86 2003
  706'.8'8—dc21

                                                          2002022086

Editor-in-Chief: Stephen Helba
Director of Production and Manufacturing: Bruce Johnson
Executive Editor: Elizabeth Sugg
Managing Editorial—Editor: Judy Casillo
Editorial Assistant: Anita Rhodes
Managing Editor—Production: Mary Carnis
Production Editor: Denise Brown
Composition: Buff Hungerland
Design Director: Cheryl Asherman
Senior Design Coordinator: Miguel Ortiz
Cover Design: Kevin Kall
Cover Printer: Phoenix Color
Printer/Binder: Banta Harrisonburg

Pearson Education LTD.
Pearson Education Australia PTY, Limited
Pearson Education Singapore, Pte. Ltd
Pearson Education North Asia Ltd.
Pearson Education Canada, Ltd.
Pearson Educación de Mexico, S.A. de C.V.
Pearson Education – Japan
Pearson Education Malaysia, Pte. Ltd
Pearson Education, Upper Saddle River, New Jersey

10 9 8 7 6 5 4 3 2 1
ISBN 0-13-097733-0

Dedication

To my students, who demand the best from me,
to Christopher, who both inspires me and frees me,
and to Crispen, Hillary, and Lizzy, who truly delight me.

Contents

An essential portion of any artist's labor is not creation so much as invocation. —Lewis Hyde

III. Graphic Presentation: Marketing Documents

As an artist, it is central to be unsatisfied! This isn't greed, though it be appetite. —Lawrence Calcagno

IV. The Interview

V. The Offer

We do not learn by experience, but by our capacity for experience.
—Buddha

VI. Addenda

Nothing is produced in a vacuum. The efforts, comments, edits, and foundation work of many are accumulated in this workbook, which I built upon with enthusiasm and appreciation. Among them:

- my family, for discussing, editing, encouraging, loving, laughing, exploring;

- my students, for complaining about sacrificed trees but faithfully pointing out needed edits, and for calling and e-mailing to report triumphs;

- faculty members, who encouraged and shared;

- the institution for which I teach, for allowing me a forum within which to stretch and the department directors who had faith that I *would* stretch to meet the demands;

- my birth family, who cherished books and art and the expressions within them;

- mentors at Desert Sun School, for demonstrating that if you had prepared your wings, you could step off the edge and fly;

- Tom Troisch, talented illustrator and animator whose drawings are in this book;

- reviewers whose insightful comments and close readings honed the manuscript, including:

  o Thomas Basmajian, The Art Institute of Philadelphia
  o Dr. Calleen Coorough, Skagit Valley College
  o Robert L. Ferro, Pittsburg State University
  o Norka Shedlock, The Art Institute of Seattle

- cover designer, Kevin Kall;

- the editorial and production team at Prentice Hall for riding herd on run–away bullets, particularly Elizabeth Sugg, Anita Rhodes, Judy Casillo, and Denise Brown;

- personal foundation work and business acumen, as included in the Resource List in the Addenda, particularly:

  o R. Bolles, *The Three Boxes of Life*
  o Kiersey and Bates, *Please Understand Me*
  o J. LeFevre, *How You Really Get Hired*
  o Tieger and Barron-Tieger, *Do What You Are*
  o J.Weinberg, *How to Win the Job You Really Want*

To those mentioned and many others, **I extend my heartfelt thanks**.

About the Author

Buff Hungerland is Academic Director for General Education at The Art Institute of Seattle. She has been an instructor for several years in the School of Design, where she has taught Design, 3-Dimensional Design, Color and Composition, Jewelry, and Design History; in the School of Fashion, where she taught Store Operations, Buying, and Leadership classes; and in General Education, where she taught English Composition and Career Development classes. She is a color consultant and makes art in both two and three dimensions. She has owned a retail store, and exhibited for 15 years in fine craft, carrying a client list of 150 galleries and stores.

Ms. Hungerland has an MA in Adult Education from Antioch University–Seattle, a K–12 Certificate in Art Education from the University of Northern Colorado, and a BA in Art History from the University of California–Riverside. Her current research interests lie in multiculturalism in design education and teaching logical/mathematical subjects to the visual/spatial student. She is passionate about design and design education and is grateful for the forum and teaching/learning exchange with her students.

Ms. Hungerland lives with her husband, an architect, and several furry creatures on an island in the Puget Sound, a short ferry ride from Seattle, Washington. She has two grown daughters, more talented than they know.

For educator support for this book, contact Buff Hungerland at www.hungerlandstudios.com. For questions to ask and stories to share, e-mail her at hungerland@earthlink.net.

About the Illustrator

Tom Troisch is an illustrator and animator of extraordinary talent. His work can be seen at www.troublefish.com.

Introduction

You've produced a
terrific portfolio.
Now what?

How do you make the leap from creating the portfolio to getting a job as a professional creative? You've worked very hard to produce a terrific portfolio, CD, demo reel, or Website. Now what?

What are the steps to take to find
- a client base or an employer whose goals are like yours,
- whose clients are interesting, and
- who appreciates the creative work you do?

Searching for a job or developing a client list is a completely different set of skills than those developed in, for instance, story boarding or art direction, nonlinear editing, or camera work. However, finding a job or developing a client list have the following segments in common with the disciplines above:
- research,
- process,
- preparation,
- completion,
- follow-up.

This workbook is for you! It is written in understandable segments to be accomplished over a quarter or a semester, to set the foundation for your career and develop skills for your life as a professional creative. It will help   you to
- set a path for yourself,
- find those interesting employers,
- make contact with them,
- prepare yourself for client and employer meetings and interviews,
- prepare marketing documents to support your interviews, and
- negotiate your financial future from strength.

You've made a considerable financial investment in your education and acquiring new skills. Now, it's time to honor that investment with a new set of skills that will help you find meaningful work in the exciting field you've chosen.

Marketing documents that represent you and provide a
platform for interviews and client presentation:
the Résumé, Sample Sheet, Cover Letter, Thank You Letter, List
of References, Letters of Recommendation, and Business Card

 You, the Corporation

Meaningful work
that supports your goals, values,
ideals, and personality through
personal integrity as an approach to
daily life, delight in and enthusiasm for
your craft, dedication to your talent,
and contribution to your community

Steps to personal
presentation:
Research, Interview Skills,
Portfolio Presentation, and
Negotiation Skills

I. The Foundation

Think of searching for a job or client base (or any task, for that matter) as *a journey*. It will be full of adventure, of situations that require you to stretch, to learn, and, like any journey worth your while, it will enrich your character. To begin your journey, you need to establish some short-term steps and long-term goals, so you know where you are on the journey. Of course, that destination might change along the way, but to give your journey some form, you need to establish some benchmarks for yourself and your corporation.

In the next segment of the workbook, we'll work together

1. to help establish your goals, and then

2. you'll imagine what your life would be like if you had *achieved* your short- and long-term goals, both professionally and personally, and finally,

3. you'll write, collage, storyboard, or render (sing, dance, perform) about the life you envision to *imprint* the positive imagery.

In **Goal Setting**, *you'll begin to think of yourself as a corporation.* Whether you work for yourself, freelance, or work for someone else, you will gain confidence and presence when *you imagine yourself working on behalf of your own corporation.* Thinking of yourself as a corporation allows you to step back from personal risk behind a shield of corporate behavior and relieves much of the anxiety of personal risk-taking.

Additionally, when you think of yourself as a corporation, whether you work for someone else (who is then your client) or for yourself, you are always thinking about corporate behavior, corporate documents, and corporate clients, rather than personal ones. It alters your outlook.

Life can only be understood backwards; but it must be lived forwards. —Soren Kirkegaard

On the **Autobiography Worksheet**, you can begin to imagine what life will be like if you attain your goals. You begin to get a sense of *the attitude and dedication it will take to achieve these goals.* World-class athletes use imaging to practice their sport over and over again. There is no reason you can't be world class, too. Imagining does *not* replace practice and dedication, but it does reinforce your skills and your commitment to your field and to your future.

On the **Reverse Autobiography Sheet** (or on your own),

- Write (or collage, storyboard, or cartoon, make a pop-up book, or perform) your autobiography, *as if you were 85 years old* and reminiscing on your life as it unfolded.

  o Include at least 5 episodes which you recall as being professionally significant and imagine them fully.

  o What did they smell, feel, sound, taste, look like? Making it *feel* real is the first step in making it real.

- Once you've "experienced" success, you can relive it or rearrange it to suit you, and when it comes (and it will, if you allow it to), you'll be ready for it with self-defeating roadblocks removed.

If I had my life to live over again...I would ride on more merry-go-rounds;
I'd pick more daisies. —Nadine Stair, age 85

Goal Setting:
Looking Forward and Planning for Success

Imagine yourself as a corporation, and fill in the blanks.

- You, the corporation (your name)

  Spectrum Graphix

- Your product or service (graphic design? interior design? toy design?)

  graphic design

- Your sales/marketing staff is

  You and everyone you know!

- Your target market (to whom will you direct your product)

  Colleges, small companies, entreprenuers

- Presentation for your market: Product Appearance (what does your work *look* like?)

  _____

- Proof of competency of product (portfolio? CD? business plan? self-promo?)

  Self-promotion

- Your corporation's **short-term goal**(s)(within the year)

  get business name out and build strong clientel

- Steps to attain these **short-term goals** (within the year)
  Plan A—Straight to your goal. Everything falls into place.
  a. _advertise, create flyers, business cards_
  b. _get clients to refer my services_

- Steps to attain the **short term goals** (within the year)
- **Plan B**—Your fall-back position. Part-time work? freelance? other jobs?
  a. _freelance_
  b. _business management_

- Your corporation's *long-term goal*(s) (5 and 10 years from now):
  5 years: _____
  10 years:_____

- Steps to attain the *long-term goals:* (Plan A)
  5 years: _____
  10 years:_____

- Steps to attain the *long-term goals:* (Plan B)
  5 years: _____
  10 years: _____

- Where will your corporation be located?_____

- Working conditions your corporation thrive in (team? with a partner? alone? active? quiet?)

  _____

- Yearly income for your corporation
  a. next year _____   b. 5 years_____

I always entertain great hopes.
—Robert Frost

```
┌ ┄ ┄ ┄ ┄ ┄ ┄ ┄ ┄ ┄ ┄ ┄ ┐
┆ Reverse Autobiography ┆
┆         Worksheet     ┆
└ ┄ ┄ ┄ ┄ ┄ ┄ ┄ ┄ ┄ ┄ ┄ ┘
```

On the following pages, construct your *reverse* autobiography, imagining what your life will be like when you achieve your goals.

Imaging: Picture it in your mind's eye. Accomplished professionals of all sorts envision the steps they'll take to accomplish their goals. So, too, will you *imagine what steps you'll take to accomplish your goals and what your life will be like as you accomplish your personal and professional goals.* Like a video of your life's story, image (*see* in your mind's eye) *yourself taking* steps to accomplish your hopes and dreams.

Plot it out: Thumbnails! In the boxes on the worksheet that follows, *plot out in phrases or pictures* where you'll be and what you'll be doing personally and professionally. When you've already set your goals for the future, *imagine* them actually happening.

- What will it feel like and look like? What will **you** look like?

- Who will be with you?

- Use *at least* 3 *professional accomplishments* in the 5 events.

Write it or **collage it, storyboard it, cartoon it, create a pop-up book, or perform it.**

- If you are in the visual or applied arts, draw it, render it, storyboard it.

- If you are in the performing arts, sing it, dance it, act it; create a performance tape, CD, or film.

Here's the scenario: You've survived to 85 years old! Wow!

1. To look back on your satisfying life, sketch (thumbnails, brainstorm, write notes) at least 9 memorable events *(the majority should be professional)* that you can relish, looking back on your life.

- Brainstorm (write) or draw thumbnail sketches in the boxes below the 9 episodes that highlight your success.

- *Note:* Don't quit at 65! You have at least 20 good productive years to live after 65. Why would you quit doing what you love to do?

2. From these 9 events below, *choose 5 events to finalize* in a 2-page paper, a storyboard or cartoon, a sequential collage, or a sequential illustration (your choice of medium). Engage your senses—what would this moment feel like, smell like, sound like, look like, taste like? Live it in your mind.

Age

60's – 80's →	retire if working for a company	stay active by volunteering scrapbooking	enjoy my grandkids
40's & 50's →	Advance in my career	Send my kids to college	plan for retirement
20's & 30's →	Establish a satisfying career	Get married and start a family	Purchase the house I plan to grow old in

```
........................
:                      :
:  Your own reverse    :
:  autobiography       :
:                      :
........................
```

Envision it! Imagine a robust and satisfying life—in detail.

- Choose 5 episodes from the Autobiography Worksheet to "re-live."
- Use all your senses to detail the image your successes throughout your life—all the way up to 85 years old! Make the journey rich.
- Use this sheet to write it, **or** collage it, storyboard it, sing it, dance it, render it, cartoon it—your choice.

Sitting on my favorite rocker on the porch of my fishing cabin, the sun warming my old bones, a laptop computer on one knee, my favorite cat curled on my shoulder, my belly full, and my face lined with life, and I think how lucky I've been.

Several writers, but particularly Richard Bolles in his work *The Three Boxes of Life* (see Resource List in the Addenda), have theorized that a productive and healthy life is made up of various components. For a professional creative, your drive and talent frame that life.

1. Personal integrity as a daily approach to life:

- The work you undertake will follow your values and ideals if you are to be fulfilled.

- Your work will need to be for companies and/or causes that you can support wholeheartedly.

- Your life's work is born of your own vision of what is valuable and is anchored by everyday actions that adhere to these values.

2. Delight in and enthusiasm for your craft:

- The work you spend your life doing should be something you *love to do*.

- When you are filled with enthusiasm, you can rise above the everyday frustrations with a full heart.

- Your enjoyment will be contagious and engaging and thus will attract the work you love.

- It's a glorious cycle that enriches you and reflects itself in the quality of the work you do.

When love and skill work together, expect a masterpiece.
—John Ruskin

3. Dedication to your talent:

- When you are full of enthusiasm for the work you do, you want to do that work well, and to explore it thoroughly.

- Who wouldn't want to keep on doing work s/he excelled at?

- You can devote yourself to doing the best you can when you work at what you love to do.

- You will grow in character and attention to detail, enjoying the depth and breadth of your life's work.

4. Contribution to your community:

- When you are full of enjoyment and full of heart,

- it is a natural next step to want to contribute to your community,

- to make the world a better, safer, more tolerant place for *all* humankind,

- this is the final step in a fulfilling and successful life.

How will you express these four components in your own life? How will you develop a wheel of enrichment that benefits you, your worklife, and the world around you?

Complete the next set of four questionnaires that follow to help identify:

1. who you are now (Keirsey Temperament Sorter or Myers-Briggs Personality Test),

2. what your values are (Values Clarification),

3. how you see your world

- Global Issues and
- Your IPO has yielded $20 Million,

4. and how that would relate to a job or client list.

Each questionnaire should be completed and its results logged onto the *Personality, Values, and Ideals Worksheet,* the next page in this section.

Complete the worksheet with question #5, by asking yourself the following:
Based on my ideals, values, and personality, what kind of workplace, company, or client would best suit me?

Finally, write, storyboard, cartoon, illustrate, collage, render at least one full page that explains what you've found out about your personality, values, and ideals, *and how that could be applied to the world of work.*

---

*An excellent resource for tying your personality type to the workplace is *Do What You Are* by Tieger and Barron–Tieger. See Resource List in the Addenda.

Personality, Values, and Ideals Worksheet

You have to leave the city of your comfort and go into the wilderness of your intuition. What you'll discover will be wonderful. What you'll discover will be yourself.
—Alan Alda

Keirsey Temperament Sorter (Sorters are but one indicator of personality and should be viewed as only a part of a whole.)

a. The results of your Keirsey Temperament Sorter or Myers-Briggs Personality Test is that you are a ___Guardian___ .

b. What does *that* mean? List major characteristics.

1. cooperative
2. concrete communicator
3. helpful
4. respectable
5. reliable
6. needs security

c. How does that apply to the world of work? List some characteristics of a compatible workplace.

1. dependable
2. easy-going
3. helpful
4. works well w/ others

Individual Values List: What were your values, according to how you perceive yourself? List below:

1. tradition
2. faith
3. religion
4. family
5. loyalty
6. accomplishment
7. God's will
8. independence
9. morality
10. discipline

Global Issues I'll Work On List: What are the most important worldwide problems you'd like to use your talents to help solve?

1. promote family
2. teach personal responsibility
3. racial + sexual issues
4. teen pregnancy
5. eliminate hunger
6. battered women
7. control political spend.
8. civil rights
9. end homelessness
10. mental health

13

Your company has gone public and your stock is now worth $20 million! What would you do with the money (keeping in mind the 4 segments of a successful life — personal integrity as a daily approach to life, delight in and enthusiasm for your craft, dedication to your talent, and contribution to your community)?

1. pay off debts
2. help family members
3. invest
4. purchase home
5. donate to schools
6. purchase car
7.
8. donate to charities
9.
10.

Everything starts as somebody's daydream. —Larry Niven

List the characteristics of a company or clients you feel would fulfill and/or match *your* personality traits and values as revealed above.

1. upbeat
2. reliable
3. laid back
4. organized
5. open-minded
6. specific
7. punctual
8. understanding
9. professional
10. realistic

Use this worksheet as the basis on which to **write, storyboard, cartoon, illustrate** *one full page* on:

1. *Who you are* and *what you value.*

2. *What do these personality traits and values mean in terms of a working environment and potential employer or freelance clients?*

```
Personality, Values,
          and Ideals
```

Using the worksheet on the previous page, write, storyboard, collage, cartoon, illustrate one full page about what you've found out about your personality, values, ideals, and finally, what kind of client or workplace or company fits with who you are.

Wow! I really found out quite a bit about myself. Of course, no one knows me like I do, but I've never thought about the relationship of my personality, values and ideals to my life's work.

The purpose of identifying your personality is to find that particular working situation in your career field that suits who you are. We'll add the results to other sorters to complete the portrait and attach that to a satisfying world of work.

┌─────────────────────────────┐
│ Sorter 1:   │
│ Keirsey Temperament Sorter │
└─────────────────────────────┘

1. Log onto the website: www.keirsey.com.

2. Take the Keirsey Temperament Sorter on line and look up your personality type as revealed by the sorter at www.ibiblio.org/personality. Choose **Personality Type Profiles**.

   - Websites change daily. If you cannot find the explanation of your personality preference profile on the Web, check out the book, *Please Understand Me*, by Keirsey & Bates at your local library or in any reputable bookstore.

3. Record your results on the Personality, Values, and Ideals Worksheet on page 12.

4. As with any of this type of sorter, the results should be *taken with a grain of salt*. These are *only indicators*, benchmarks which should be personally illuminating for you, your partners, and significant others. They do **not**, however, *completely* define anyone.

5. Have fun! Why not have your significant other take it too?

*Resource: *Please Understand Me* by Keirsey & Bates. Other interesting work relating personality type to work and careers is done by Tieger & Barron-Tieger. See Resource List included in the Addenda.

*Another personality sorter is the *Myers-Briggs Personality Test*. Both Keirsey & Bates and Myers-Briggs are based on Jungian psychology. Both are psychologically sound and professionally accepted, but no matter what type of personality test you take, it can only give you *part* of the picture explaining the unique person you are.

Highlight *all* the values you hold most dear. Add your own in the margin or at the end. **From those highlighted**, *choose 10 to place on the* **Personality, Values, and Ideals Worksheet.**

accomplishment	achievement	activity	admiration
advancement	advantage	adventure	affection
affluence	ambition	appearance	artistic expression
athletics	authenticity	authority	autonomy
beauty	belonging	brotherhood	business
career	caring	challenge	change
chaos	charity	clarity	close friends
comfort	commitment	competition	conformity
connection	conservation	consistency	contentment
control	cooperation	country	country living
creativity	credit	culture	
decisiveness	discipline	docility	dominance
drama	duty		
economic security	education	employment	endurance
energy	enjoyment	enterprise	entertainment
entrepreneurship	environment	equal opportunity	eternal life
excitement	exercise	experimentation	exploration
faith	fame	family	flamboyance
freedom	friendship	fresh ideas	frivolity
fun			
God's will	Golden Rule	goodness	graciousness
happiness	healing	health	helping
holiness	home	honesty	honor
hope	humility	humor	

imagination	impulse	income	independence
individualism	industriousness	inner direction	inner harmony
innovation	integrity	intellectual	intimacy
involvement			
joviality	joy		
lack of pretense	laughter	leadership	leisure
literature	love	loyalty	
managing	mastery	materialism	maturity
meditation	mentoring	modesty	money
morality			
nature	neatness	nonconformity	nurturing
obedience	order		
patience	peace	persistence	philanthropy
physical power	pleasure	politics	possessions
production	professionalism	prosperity	psychic power
reading	rebellion	recognition	recreation
religion	reputation	respect	responsibility
retirement	rewards	riches	
satisfaction	schedule	security	sensuality
sincerity	spirituality	stability	stamina
status	stimulation	success	survival
taking risks	teamwork	tenacity	tolerance

touch   tradition   tranquility   travel
trust   truth

understanding

wealth   wisdom

zest   zeal

Others you've thought of:

*Resource built upon: Simon et al. *Values Clarification, A Handbook for Practical Strategies.* See Resource List included in the Addenda.

What **Global Issue**s would you like to contribute your time, energy, and creativity to help solve (*pro bono* work)? **Highlight all** those which you value, *add your own* in the margins or at the end, and then **transfer** 10 of them to the **Personality, Values, and Ideals Worksheet** on page 13.

- find suitable families worldwide for orphans of war

- promote small and individual businesses

- clone human beings

- continue stem-cell research

- eliminate chemical addictions

- support the right to die

- eliminate racial, sexual, and sexual preference discrimination

- promote equal opportunity for all humans

- nurture marriage and family enrichment

- fund country-wide free health care

- promote affordable leisure activities

- fund free post-secondary education

- support creative flex-time work hours

- elevate pay for day-care and elder-care workers

- fund free, quality day-care for children and elders

- eliminate pesticides, miticides, herbicides, and fungicides from the food chain

- forbid the use of heavy metals used as fertilizers on food crops

- prohibit the use of heavy metals in fertilizers

- defeat genetic diseases and cancers

- recycle resources

- reduce world population

- control political spending

- fund free pet neutering

- fund free human birth control

- promote distance and remote learning for degrees

- support waste control of spent fuels, heavy metals

- eliminate hunger worldwide

- help develop jobs and enterprise to reduce poverty

- everyone shares equally in the nation's defense

- fund climate control research to avoid famine

- promote the removal of land mines

- treat tobacco and marijuana equally

- utilize the expertise of elders

- share knowledge/skills with the community

- promote trading communities to equalize wealth

- equalize standard of living throughout the world

- care of children as community effort

- conquer viral plagues (AIDS, ebola, hantavirus, etc.)

- promote the use of solar energy and alternative fuels

- support universal multilingual and multicultural education

- contribute to the conservation of fossil fuels

- practice religious tolerance

- end physical and psychological family abuse

- develop efficient, safe public transit

- promote care of the family as a community effort

- create meaningful work for all

- abolish capital punishment

- promote *people-skills* education

- end homelessness

- develop a 1-page tax return for all

- teach personal responsibility

- recycle abandoned housing

- Other global issues important to you:

*This section was inspired by Richard Bolles work in *The Three Boxes of Life*. See Resource List in the Addenda at the end of this book.

¡¡ *YIPPEE* !!

Your internet start-up company has lasted through the down-turn, gotten solid backing, and has just gone public. Your reward for hanging in there is your stock in the company is now worth

$20 million!

***Now* what are you going to do** to maintain a worthwhile and fulfilling life, keeping in mind that satisfaction comes from
- *personal integrity*,
- *delight in your craft*,
- *dedication to your talent*, and
- *contribution to your community.*

Use your choices below to fill in your **Personality, Values, and Ideals Worksheet.**

1. Pay off all my credit cards

2. Pay off my mother's credit cards

3. Buy a beautiful house, big enough for when I start a family

In every adult there lurks a child - an eternal child, something that is always becoming, is never completed, and calls for unceasing care, attention, and education. That is the part of the human personality which wants to develop and become whole. —C. G. Jung

4. Move my grandmother out of New York and get her a place
5. Help any struggling family member

6. Donate to a church who I know will use the money for good use
7. Start my own company
8.

9.

10.

Note: There are no *good* choices or *bad* choices in any of these sorters, just **your** choices.

*This section built upon Richard Bolles work in *The Three Boxes of Life*. See Resource List in the Addenda at the end of this book.

Designing how much time you spend on each of your activities helps you frame your life's work. *You* are the one who decides how you spend your time, but each of us can get caught up in daily life and lose sight of our values, ideals, and goals.

It can be very revealing to find out how you spend your time each day right now. When it is clear what you'd **like** to do with your time as opposed to what you're doing now, *you can implement some changes* to coincide with your values, ideals, and goals. Then you can be *proactive* in your time management (which puts you in control of your use of time) rather than *reactive* (which puts you at the mercy of the demands of an active career).

Part I: Proposed Time Management

- To determine how you'd like to be spending your time each week, divide the circle at the left into the **4 categories** that follow to represent how much of your week you'd like to devote to each category.

- This plan can be a projection for the future or for next week, as you choose.

Category I: sharpening skills

- o day and night school, classes on the Internet
- o studying, homework
- o reading and researching on the Internet
- o seminars, workshops, skills upgrades
- o getting there (transportation)

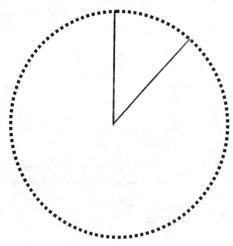

Time is the coin of your life. It is the only coin you have, and only you can determine how it will be spent. Be careful lest you let other people spend it for you. —Carl Sandburg

Category II: employing skills

- o full-time job
- o part-time job
- o volunteer work
- o freelance work from your own studio
- o getting there (transportation)

Category III: hanging out

- o watching TV
- o computer games, Internet games
- o hanging out with family, friends, loved ones
- o physical games and sports
- o reading for fun

Category IV: keeping it together

- o cooking and eating meals
- o sleeping
- o bathing, grooming, dressing
- o exercise
- o household chores, errands and shopping

Part II. Actual Time Management

To determine how much of your life you actually devote to each of the 4 sections, **keep a daily log** on page 29, noting how many hours you devoted to each activity. It is *important* to keep this log *every day* to get some meaningful information from it. You lose the subtleties of your current time management if you try to backtrack more than one day.

When you've completed your daily log, fill in the circle on the left with the results.

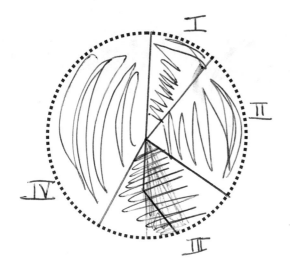

Part III. Comparing *Proposed* Time Management with *Actual* Time Management

Compare your *proposed time management* circle with your *actual time management* circle. Then write at least 3 paragraphs, using the sheet following the Time Log, (or collage, storyboard, cartoon 3 segments) on **three time management issues** you've found in detailing the results of your weekly log, and **what you can do to implement changes** to make your life coincide with your values, ideals, and goals.

*This section was inspired by a time management segment in Richard Bolles' excellent book, *The Three Boxes of Life*. See Resource List in the Addenda.

Designing Your Time
Daily Log

	M	T	W	R	F	S	Su
Sharpening Skills Day/night school, classes on Internet Studying/homework Reading, researching on the Net Seminars, workshops, skills upgrades Getting there (transportation)	no work	2hrs 5hrs 25min	4HRS 25min				
Employing Skills Full-time job Part-time job Volunteer work Freelance work in your own studio Getting there (transportation)	4 hours 30 minutes	no work 5min						
Hanging Out Watching TV Computer games, Internet games Hanging out with friends, family Physical games/sports Reading for fun		5hrs						
Keeping It Together Cooking and eating Sleeping Bathing, grooming, dressing Exercise Household chores, errands, shopping		1Hrs. 2HRS						
Weekly Total								

Once you've compared your *proposed* with your *actual* time management, write, collage, or storyboard your decisions about how you'll change your behavior to manage your time. Concentrate on 3 time management issues you've uncovered.

"I never thought about controlling my time, especially when much of it seems to be already set for me! Here's what I found out:

...and that's what I'm going to do to manage my time to coincide with my values, ideals, and goals."

Stress Management

People are always blaming their circumstances for what they are. I don't believe in circumstances. The people who get on in this world are the people who get up and look for the circumstances they want, and, if they can't find them, make them.

—*George Bernard Shaw, 1893*

Changes *of any kind* are stressful. When you are graduating from school, changing jobs, or soliciting clients, changes are inevitable. It's important to develop *some strategies to maintain your health and balanced outlook* while you are making changes in your life.

Here are some strategies (add new ones to the end of the list):

1. Breathe deeply (really!) and slowly now and then to relax and refill your system with oxygen.

2. Do something each day that delights you.

3. Reward yourself when you've completed each task (and of course, limit your tasks to those which can *actually* be completed.)

4. Exercise regularly—at least 3 times a week for 20 minutes.

5. Practice saying "No" so that you can employ "No" when appropriate.

6. Give at least one compliment to others a day.

7. Go on a journey to a calm center-place within you each day for 5 minutes. Maybe it is bathed in your favorite color. Bask in the light. Breathe in the light. Meditate there in that safe and beautiful place.

8. Relish change as a challenge to your creativity and ingenuity.

9. Honor the child within yourself and within others.

10. Concentrate on the task at hand. Finish it. Breathe deeply. Move on to the next task.

11. Respond to your mail when you receive it.

12. Take a 5-minute break at least once an hour. Get up and walk around.

13. Delegate responsibly.

14. Lead by acting in a way others can emulate.

15. Once a day, listen to the silence between sounds.

16. Construct a positive attitude.

17. Cultivate a positive support system.

18. Release your need to respond to negative people.

19. Open your existence to beneficial inputs.

20. Allow yourself to be silly and laugh out loud at least once a day.

21. Give up responsibility for other people's reactions.

22. Savor at least one act you've done well each day.

23. Others you've thought of:

Financial Management

In this segment, we'll determine what kind of yearly salary you need *to maintain present obligations* and *plan for the future*, so you know *what you can accept in salary*, or how many freelance jobs you need to obtain to fulfill your financial needs and to live and work according to your *values, ideals, and goals.*

Here is the procedure for taking charge of your Financial Management:

1. Fill in Monthly Financial Projections **(Sheet A)** fully **IN PENCIL**.

   - Use your checkbook, debit statement, or financial records as a resource to fill in as many blanks as possible.

   - Remember, this is a *typical* month.

   - If you live at home, ask a friend or check the newspaper for expense information (apartment ads, food ads, etc.)

2. Fill in **Financial Plan Sheet (Sheet B)** to determine how much per month must be put toward saving for big-ticket items (a computer, for instance, or new software) and to pay off debt.

   - What do you have for your one-year goals?
     Pay off credit card? Vacation? Investments? Computer?

   - How about your 5-year goal?
     New equipment? Your own business? Down payment on a new car?

   - 15 years from now?
     Pay off schooling? Advanced degree? Down payment on a house?
     Medical costs to have a child?

   - **Note**: If you find that your plans require too high a monthly set-aside, you can adjust the number of years or adjust the down-payment required.

We act as though comfort and luxury were chief requirements of life, when all that we need to make us happy is something to be enthusiastic about.
—*Charles Kingsley*

3. Bring totals from both

   - **Monthly Financial Projections (Sheet A)** and
   - **Financial Planning (Sheet B)** to the chart below:

4. Complete the box below **in pencil:**

Wages and Salary Box

1. Total Monthly Expenses $285   **Sheet A**

2. Total Monthly Savings and Payoffs   _____ + **Sheet B**

3. = Total Monthly Net (Take-home)   _____ = Net (take-home pay)

4. Complement of Tax and SS (see next section)   _____ % = _____ (decimal)

5. Divide Net (#3) by Complement (#4) to arrive at Gross Monthly Income_____ Gross Monthly Income

6. Multiply Gross Monthly Income (#5 above) by 12 months to arrive at **Gross Yearly Income** _____

This is the **gross salary** you'll need to earn to take home (net) enough (after taxes and Social Security are taken out) to meet your financial obligations and savings goals. (See Glossary in the Addenda for definition of *gross salary*.)

The aim of art, the aim of life can only be to increase the sum of freedom and responsibility to be found in every person and in the world. —Albert Camus

5. **Whew!** You *might* need to cut back on some projected obligations.

   - Will you skip some entertainment? New clothes?

   - Transportation—sell car or take public transportation?

   - Move in with some friends to cut back on rent?

   - Do you need to cut back on your short- and medium-term goals? Or change them from 5 years to 7 years?

   - Or do you need to arrange for a 2nd job or freelance clients to meet your projected obligations?

6. **Rework** the sheet until *your expenses* (obligations) *and projected savings match a realistic income*. Here's where the *pencil* comes in handy!

Typical Monthly Expenses	
Rent or house payment	600
Utilities (cable, electricity, gas, garbage)	600
Food and household goods	200 20
Transportation costs	50 40
Car insurance	
Health insurance	
Renters or homeowners insurance	
Other insurance (dental, glasses, disability)	
Day care (child or elder)	
Clothing allowance	30 40
Entertainment allowance	
Supplies (school, office, art)	
Phone/Internet	30 50
Household or transportation maintenance	
Other credit cards	135
Other	
Other	
Other	
Total Monthly Expenses (Sheet A)	= 285
transfer to #1 in the Salary Box on page 34	

Sheet A: Monthly Financial Projections

1. Fill in a *typical* month.

2. Transfer total monthly expenses to the **Salary Box** on page 34.

100,000 house

Sheet B: Financial Planning

- This is a financial plan (monthly savings) for *planned purchases and pay-offs* that allows you freedom to anticipate future *needs.* Financial planning changes your outlook from *reactive* to *proactive* and helps you live according to your values, ideals, and goals.

- List the items you want to acquire (down payment on a house, car, etc.), estimate the total amount, and divide by the months required. Complete in PENCIL as *many adjustments may have to be made.*

  For instance, if you want to accumulate the down-payment on a house (say, $10,000) in the next 5 years, you'd need to save ($10,000 divided by 60 [12 x 5] months), or $167 per month for the next 5 years.

Nine out of ten rich men of our country today, started out in life as poor boys, with determined wills, industry, perseverance, economy, and good habits. —P.T. Barnum

1. Item	2. Total	3. Monthly Payment
Short-Term Goals: 1 year (12 months)—divide Total (col. 2) by 12		
Verizon Visa	$ 800	$ 67
Capital One	$ 200	$ 17
Belk's	$ 600	$ 50
Medium-Term Goals: 5 years (60 months)—divide Total (col. 2) by 60		
GMC Yukon	$ 30,000	$ 500
	$	$

Pay off credit (handwritten, left margin)

680 (handwritten)

4 (handwritten)

Long-Term Goals: 15 years (180 months)—divide Total (col. 2) by 180

House	$200,000	$1,111
	$	$

Total Financial Planning Savings (total monthly payments)
(transfer to **Salary Box** line for **Sheet B** on page 34) $_____

Part I: Complements

- Complements: *together total 100%, so*

    o 45% (.45) is the complement to 55% (.55)
    o 60% (.60) is the complement to 40% (.40)
    o 15% (.15) is the complement to 85% (.85), etc.

- *Complements* are used

    o *in retail* to go from gross to net (or wholesale to retail),
    o and net to gross, which is exactly what you do when you figure your gross salary and your take-home pay.
    o They are also used to calculate profit and overhead margins.
    o They are very versatile and help you remain financially solvent.
    o Just like an airbrush or a pencil or a boom-box, *a complement is a tool* used to figure percentages of increase or decrease (or the relationship of gross to net pay).

Part II: Terms
- gross: total salary *without* taxes and Social Security removed
- net: take-home pay, salary *with* taxes and Social Security removed

Part III: Gross to net

- to get from the large figure (gross yearly salary) to the small figure (net or take-home pay), you *multiply* by the complement

- ☑ **To calculate gross to net: *multiply* by the complement**

- so, if you are offered a salary of $20,000
    o and you want to know if that will provide *enough take home pay* (after taxes and Social Security are taken out)
    o to cover your anticipated needs (say $1500 per month),
    o *multiply* the salary by your tax and Social Security complement.

a. Figure your tax and Social Security complement

7.84%   Social Security employee's contribution

<u>17.00%</u>   Federal Income Tax bracket (hypothetical)

24.84%   Income tax and Social Security withholding

100.00%   = 1.0000

<u>-   24.84%</u>   <u>= - .2484</u>

75.16%   = .7516

b. $20,000 salary offered
<u>   x .7516 (tax and S.S. complement)</u>
$15,032 net (take-home pay—after withholding taxes
and Social Security

- Compare that to your expenses and see if you can afford to take the job. Say
you need $1,500 per month net to cover expenses and savings:

$ 1,500 per month expenses
<u>   x 12 months</u>
$18,000 yearly expenses to cover with net pay

$ 15,070 net (take-home pay) as calculated above
<u>- 18,000 expenses</u>
$ - 2,930 *shortfall* **(oops!)**

- **Ack! You can't afford to take this job!** What next?
  o   cut down on expenses
  o   take freelance jobs on the side (only if you have not signed a "do-not-
      compete" contract…)
  o   negotiate a higher salary

Part IV: Net to gross

1. You know your expenses and financial planning are projected to be $1,500 per month or ($1,500 x 12 months): $18,000 per year.

2. You now calculate the **net to gross** (small to large) to figure out *how much you have to earn in gross salary to take home enough net salary to cover your expenses and financial planning.*

3. What salary or total of freelance jobs must you take to cover these projected needs and goals?

☑ **To calculate net to gross: Divide by the complement.**

4. $18,000 ÷ .7516 = $23,948.91

5. You need almost $24,000 *gross salary* to have enough net pay (take-home pay) to cover your $18,000 yearly expenses.

Part V: Hourly wage

☑ **To calculate an gross yearly wage based on an hourly wage, begin by *multiplying* hours x wages to equal *gross* wages.**

1. First calculate how many hours are worked in a year:

2. 40 [hours/week] x 52 [weeks/ year] = 2080 [hours/year]

3. Next, multiply your hourly wage by 2080

4. Say you're offered a job for $15 per hour full-time.

   - $15/hour x 2080 hours per year = $31,200 gross yearly wages

   - What is the *take-home (net) pay?*

- $31,200 x .7516 = $23,449.92 take-home (net) pay

- *Remember*, federal income tax percentages increase as your income increases. Social Security contributions remain the same (15.68%)—a constant changed only by Congress.

Part VI: Freelance

- You don't want to sell your own work or market on your own behalf?
  - *Question:* When can you afford to hire a sales representative?
  - *Answer:* when *you* don't have time to do the marketing because you are so busy doing your creative work

- You have a sales representative or agent or agency
  - S/he will take 20% (for instance) of the *gross sales* of your work as her/his fee.
  - Fee percentages are a matter of *negotiation.*

- How will you figure out when you're making enough to cover your projected expenses and financial planning?

- You are in our familiar 17% tax bracket.
  - You have the familiar *employee's* share of the Social Security withholding: 7.84%
  - *You **also** have the employer's* share of the Social Security withholding because you work for yourself: another 7.84%.

  - So: 17% + 0 + 7.84% + 7.84% = 32.68%
  - To arrive at your *complement*, take 32.68% from 100%

$$
\begin{array}{ccc}
100.00\% & = & 1.00 \\
- \ 32.68\% & = & - .3268 \\
\hline
67.32\% & = & .6732
\end{array}
$$

Now you have a tool to figure out your net (take home) fee:

- You're offered a free lance job for $2,000

- Your rep takes 20% (find the complement) = 80% = .8

1. $2,000 x .8 = $1,600
   - this is the gross amount **you** pay tax on
   - the rep pays on his/her $400

2. $1600 x .6732 = $1077.12
   - this is your *take-home (net) fee* to cover expenses and financial planning

3. $522.88 ($1600 – $1077.12) goes into your business savings account for taxes and Social Security payments which are
   - Often due quarterly for the self-employed.
   - **Do not skip saving for taxes or paying them.**

Wage/ Math Tips

1. Complement: tax and Social Security multiplier (add taxes and Social Security contribution, subtract from 100% [or 1.00] to arrive at complement, change % into a decimal)

2. Net to gross (small to large): *Divide* by complement

3. Gross to Net (large to small): *Multiply* by complement

4. Hourly wage: *Multiply* by 2080 (hr/yr)

Part VII: Additional Notes

- *If you live in a state which has a **state income tax**, you simply **add** that state tax to the federal tax and Social Security* to arrive at the figure from which to derive the complement.

- Social Security is a constant (does not graduate with income as does income tax), mandated by Congress. However, Congress changes its percentages from time to time.

  - Everyone who works in the United States contributes 7.84% of their paycheck to Social Security up to a certain percentage of total income.

  - Every employer contributes a matching amount.

  - *If you are working freelance (self-employed), you are **both the employee and employer**, and your contribution to Social Security is 15.68%.* This may also hold true if you are working *on contract* (determined by whether you obtain the jobs yourself or through an agency—make sure you find out who is responsible for tax and Social Security payments).

- *Stay current* on local, state, and federal tax information. Ignorance is not an excuse for disobeying the law. Check with your accountant or *tax information hotline* (under "Government" in your phone book) for up-to-date information on taxes in your state.

- **This segment *IS intended* to give you a *general overview* of regulations and instruments to calculate your salary, fees, and wages. It is *NOT intended* to be a *substitute for sound financial* advice from a licensed professional.**

II. The Marketplace

The **marketplace** is where buyers and sellers of goods and services meet. Your goal is to *anticipate* the needs of the marketplace so you can supply services to the most beneficial buyer for you (and your corporation).

- There are jobs and marketing opportunities in each of these sectors. It is important to understand the **form of the marketplace** so you can identify where an opportunity lies that coincides with your goals, values and ideas.

- Each of these sectors can supply a client base, as they *ALL* need public relations and posters created, Websites maintained, meetings planned, brochures produced, offices remodeled, ergonomic furniture designed, and workplace safety CDs created, among many other design-related services rendered.

The marketplace has three sectors:

1. The **Private Sector** (organizations which intend to make a profit), has two parts: **publicly held**, and **privately held**.

   a. **Publicly held:** owned by a group of individuals, traded publicly on one of several stock exchanges.

   Example: General Electric, Cisco, Boeing, Microsoft, Amazon.com

   These are companies which issue stock that can be bought by the public. The stock is usually traded on some part of the stock market (New York Stock Exchange, American Stock Exchange, NASDAQ, among others).

   These companies must disclose their financial dealings to their stockholders in year-end (annual) reports. These companies are therefore good prospects for the graphic designer because the production of such reports must be designed and printing organized.

b. Privately held: owned by an individual or group of individuals; ownership closed to the public

Example: The Seahawks Football Team

Stock may have been issued, but it is closely held by a private group and is not publicly traded.

No financial disclosure must be made, and therefore, marketing of graphic design services is limited to advertising, signage, corporate identity, etc. No annual reports.

Job Watch for the **Private Sector:**

- Security is low in the private sector

- Opportunity to advance and to the entrepreneur, however, is **high**

- Highest job mobility (you can move from job to job *within* this sector)

- Highest salary opportunities

2. **The Non-Profit Sector** is made up of organizations which may not make a profit, but which are intend to promote well-being in some way. They are generally funded by grants and donations, and are called NPOs—Non-Profit Organizations. This sector includes educational and cultural institutions, foundations and charities, social services agencies, and hospitals.

Example: The Red Cross, United Way, Greenpeace, Public Broadcasting Service, National Public Radio, Seattle Art Museum

Recent development in this sector has some types of organizations, which are *traditionally* a part of this sector, such as hospitals, and some educational institutions, moving to the *private sector*.

Job Watch for **the Non-Profit Sector:**

- Low job security as these institutions are dependent on funding packages of various sorts which must be renewed, and may be politically tied.

- Less mobility than in the private sector as there are fewer jobs in this category.

- There is a great deal of *job satisfaction* in "helping" jobs.

- Salaries are relatively low.

3. **The Public Sector** includes the many forms of government, funded by the citizenry for its benefit. Do not confuse the *publicly held* part of the private sector with the *public sector*.

These are usually *government* jobs, created to promote the greater good for the people under its jurisdiction, such as: mayor, police, street and park maintenance, policy and political jobs, city, county, state, and federal agencies. There is a structured work environment and clientele.

Example: national, state, and local governments, public education, police and state patrol, road and bridge construction and maintenance, national parks, national defense, emergency preparedness, etc.

Job Watch for the **Public Sector:**

- Security is high as it is difficult to fire anyone in the Public Sector.

- Salaries are moderate (raises are tied to political negotiation).

- Less mobility than in the private sector because the relative number of jobs is smaller.

*Resource built upon: *How to Win the Job You Really Want,* pp. 205 — 206, by Janice Weinberg. See Resource List included in the Addenda.

Each company, small or large, has certain divisions or functions. Yours does too. These divisions each have a job to do for the corporation.

Typical divisions or functions within an organization:

- **design of a product or service** (creating ideas, concepts, and potential products)

- **marketing, advertising, and sales** (presentation of product/service to intended target market)

- **manufacture** of product (overseeing, managing, fabrication of product)

- **delivery** of product/service (warehousing, picking, labeling, packing, boxing, and trucking)

- **strategic planning** for future stance in the marketplace

- **management of daily financial activities** (payroll, paydown of debt, bill paying, returns)

- **facilities management** and real estate acquisition (building management, cleaning, rent, and acquisition of new sites)
- **public relations** (representation of organization to the public)

- **human resources** (staffing, insurance, 401K and retirement, investment packages, safety, etc.)

- **legal affairs** (managing the company's legal issues)

These functions may be accomplished *by one person as in a sole proprietorship*; that is, one person directs or even performs each function. You will also be performing these functions (or hiring someone to see that they are performed) for your own studio.

Why is this important to you?

- In a large company, *separate functions are carried out by separate departments.*

- ***Each of these departments may have its own budget and is therefore an independent** target market **for the savvy practitioner of visual, applied, and media arts.***

How can you market to each of the following divisions (functions)?

Identify a way you (your corporation) could market your skills to *each* of the following functions of an organization.

Example*:* A **Graphic Designer** could develop a signage and collateral program:

- *in Delivery (boxes, tags, bags);*

- *in Human Resources (folders and presentation packages, parties and awards);*

- *to Public Relations for advertising layout and graphics;*

- *formatted forms for Strategic Planning;*

- *safety and directional signage for Facilities Management;*

- *flow charts, procedural signs for Manufacture;*

- *presentation folders for Legal Affairs, etc.*

Your turn: Your specialty: <u>Graphics/Business Major</u>

How could you market to:

- Design: ———————————————————————

- Marketing/Sales: ————————————————————

- Manufacturing: ——————————————————————

- Delivery of Product: ——————————————————

- Strategic Planning: ————————————————————

- Financial Management (day-to-day activities): _____

- Facilities Management and Real Estate Acquisition:
  ———————————————————————————————————

- Public Relations: ——————————————————————

- Human Resources (Personnel): ———————————————

- Legal Affairs: ————————————————————————

*Resource built upon: *How to Win the Job You Really Want,* p. 206, by Janice Weinberg.   See Resource List included in the Addenda.

Trends in Your Industry

In each sector, but particularly in the Private (for-profit) Sector, whole industries and businesses work their way through a *standard life cycle* that includes four stages:

1. **Birth,**
2. **Growth,**
3. **Maturity,**
4. **Death**.

Business in general is dynamic and always changing. The movement and change of industry and businesses within each industry represent **trends.**

- Where is any segment or category of business going? in 3 years? in 5 years? in 10 years?

- What has changed *in the last 3 years*?

There are career opportunities, in terms of jobs and clients, and disadvantages as well, within each of the industry life stages.

1. **Birth***:* These are industries just being born, businesses which are just being thought of today.

   - You might not even be aware of them yet, nor of the technologies being developed to support them. The communications industry is full of ideas just being born. Venture capital places its money here.

   - The birth stage can also include new niches in a mature marketplace, such as the birth of keyboards meeting computing needs from the dying typewriter industry, or further advances such as skate wheels inside the sole of athletic shoes.

- New communications niches are born daily. New ideas, products, and services are born as well. These businesses, if they survive this stage, move rapidly to the growth stage. Do you have a niche worth exploring?

- *Job security* in birth businesses is unpredictable, but the *opportunity for growth is huge*. There are many jobs in this category for job changers, students, and new entries into the market. The birth state is a place that is youth oriented, but experience also counts and is leaned upon. You may be offered part of the company in lieu of high pay, or profit share in lieu of benefits.

- Flexibility and willingness to work long hours are prized. If you are *risk oriented*, this is the place for you.

2. **Growth:** These are businesses which have survived the birth stage and have begun growing and expanding.

- The limits have not been explored. There has been a recent "shake-out" or "correction" where a business category is overoccupied with product or couldn't deliver on its promises or product, but the dip seems to have been short-lived and has injected a dose of reality in these rapidly growing companies.

- It's a ***youth-oriented*** market. You'll need ***time*** (**lots**) invested in this segment. Expect to work for a fixed salary and give plenty (60+ hours per week, on average) of **time**.

- Businesses on the *Internet*, software programs, or computer gaming are in the growth stage, even with the recent correction in the marketplace. *If you work on contract in this segment, be aware that the work can be seasonal and the contracts short-term.*

- *Job security* is better than in the birth stage, and the opportunity for promotion is enormous. There are many jobs available in this phase, as the companies are growing and expanding.

3. **Maturity:** In this stage, a type of business has been around a long time, and while sales might not be growing at an incredible rate, there is a good solid base for slow *controlled* growth. Mergers and acquisitions happen often in this category.

- Examples?

    a. Boeing is an example of a mature company and has merged with another large aero-space company.

    b. Computer *hardware* companies are moving into a mature phase. Remember the tan boxes; those unattractive bulky desk hogs that used to house computers? As computers got faster and faster, they sold no matter what they looked like. When they got to be cool looking so they'd sell, that was a sign that the market had matured. (This is ripe territory for *industrial designers!*)

- Jobs are usually stable in this category, although d*ownsizing (right-sizing), reorganization*, and *outsourcing* affect this category. Reorganization, however, and outsourcing are parts of this category which offer opportunity for entrepreneurs, as clients and as niche start-ups.

- As a job changer, new entrant into the market, or a student, you might have to wait for someone to retire before finding a place in this category. *Consultants* (who have experience, but have been right-sized or downsized out of their middle management positions) often come from this category of industry.

- You must remember, however, that if a mature company is your employer or major client, you *always* represent *your own "corporation,"* and you must be on the lookout for approaching downsizing and other strategies that affect the short-term "bottom line." Keep your networking contacts current.

4. **Death**: This is a category in which a company, category, or type of business has been overwhelmed by the marketplace, or its product outstripped by something new.

- Examples?

    a. Typewriters and rotary phones, beta videos, eight–track tapes. When was the last time you saw a new one marketed except at a flea market or on *e–bay*?

    b. Many small "Mom & Pop" stores go out of business because a superstore can provide so much more inventory (not *service*, however, which is where small stores can fight such take-overs in their market).

- Jobs are usually not available for job changers, students, and those who are just entering the job market. However, *repositioning* dying industries or businesses in the marketplace—from typewriters to keyboards, for instance—(back into the growth stage) requires new capital, a new product, new marketing strategies, and possibly **you** and your services!

*Resource built upon: *How You Really Get Hired,* p. 24, by John LaFevre. See Resource List included in the Addenda.

A Trend Report is basically an Informational Interview extended, in which you ask about current trends and changes in the marketplace rather than about how your interviewee got started in business. Sure, you can combine both.

■ With a group of friends or classmates in your field, *brainstorm the trends* in your area of interest (this can be products, types of services, specific companies, new materials, "looks," etc.). Fill in the following blanks:

1. Your Industry or Professional Practice (Graphic Design, Industrial Design, Interior Design, etc.) :

   Graphic Design

2. Areas in that field that are in the **Birth Stage**:

   a.

   b.

   c.

3. Areas in that field that are in the **Growth Stage (what's hot now)**:

   a.

   b.

   c.

4. Areas in that field that are in the **Maturity Stage:**

    a.

    b.

    c.

5. Areas in that field which are in the **Death Stage:**

    a.

    b.

    c.

Informational Interview for Trend Report:

Now prepare for an Informational Interview (see **Informational Interview** techniques in **Networking** section of this book). Instead of focusing on questions about how to get started as you might in your Lead I's (see **Networking** section of this book), now you'll ask about **trends** in the marketplace:

1. What has changed in the last 3–5 years?

2. What is happening now?

3. What does your interviewee see as coming trends—business, product, technique, software, client base, etc.—anything looming out on the horizon in terms of your type of business?

4. How should you prepare yourself for coming changes in the marketplace?

Research: *Before you contact anyone, it is important that you do your research* first as you would for any Lead I. See the **Networking** section of this book for hints on how to conduct an informational interview and how to do research on your subject.

Questionnaire: List some *open-ended questions to ask* (those which start a conversation, and which cannot be answered with one word—See the Networking section of this book). Fill these in and *be prepared* for the informational interview:

1.

2.

3.

4.

_____   A thank you note has been written and sent to the person
(check)   you interviewed.

Organizing your *written* Trend Report (1 + pages):

1. Introduction: Who you called and why

2. The meat of the paper: What I asked, and the answers.

3. Conclusion: Your analysis of the answers, given what I know about your industry

4. Any visuals you can collect that will help your audience identify the interviewee.

Notes for the *oral* presentation of your paper (3–5 minutes):

1. I interviewed _____

   from _____

   (company name)

   because: _____

2. Questions you asked and answers you received:

   Q:
   A:

   Q:
   A:

Q:
A:

3. Conclusions you've drawn:

4. Any questions from the audience?

5. Thank you. (Pick up your visual examples and exit with grace.)

Write it (storyboard it, cartoon it, collage it):

The marketplace changes really quickly! Things are not the same as they were 5 years ago. Here's what I've found out.

```
┌ ▪▪▪▪▪▪▪▪▪▪▪▪▪▪▪▪▪▪▪▪▪ ┐
  Related Fields and
        Job Map
└ ▪▪▪▪▪▪▪▪▪▪▪▪▪▪▪▪▪▪▪▪▪ ┘
```

A **job map** is an exploration of *the direct path to your goal as well as alternatives to that direct path*. Ancillary industries (support industries) offer terrific opportunities to new entries and career changers, especially if your new training is in cutting-edge technologies such as the newest software or its direct application.

- Have you become an expert in a new software application? Do you like interaction with people? Are you a self-starter? Maybe a sales position with a software manufacturer is perfect for you. Travel, adventure, bucks!

- Or you could use both your design skills and software application skills to train the staff already in-house with a company in applying design skills to a new software.

- Or you could be on a demonstration team with the software, product application, or manufacturing company.

People are all alike in their promises. It is only in their deeds that they differ.
—Moliere

Complete the next segment to explore *your own interesting options.* Try to keep an open mind and your eyes on the long-term prize. On the sheet that follows (see example sheet filled in)

1. **List the steps to the top of your particular profession,**

    - for instance, from the top down:

        a. producer,
        b. assistant producer,
        c. creative director,
        d. art director,
        e. assistant art director,
        f. animator,
        g. ink and painter.

    - for instance, from the bottom up:

        a. materials librarian,
        b. color board construction and replication,
        c. drafter,
        d. assistant designer,
        e. designer,
        f. project manager,
        g. associate,
        h. partner.

2. **Identify those positions which might be support in nature:**
   Paper sales if you are a graphic designer; or plastic mold-making material sales if you are an industrial designer; software demonstration for many design disciplines, etc.

3. **Identify companies or agencies from different segments of the market (public, private, not-for-profit),** that might hold promise as places that might hire you full-time or that might be a good group for a client base from which to prospect for leads.

4. **Put this information on the Job Map that follows to help guide your search for leads and your career path.**

```
. . . . . . . . . . . . . . . .
.                              .
:  Job Map                     :
.                              .
. . . . . . . . . . . . . . . .
```

Life has some crazy twists and turns.

- To take advantage of the opportunities that challenge you, plot your direct career path (Plan A), and then plot other possibilities that use your skills and help you to achieve a satisfying career. This will help you remain open to the possibilities as they present themselves, rather than remaining stuck in a narrow focus.

- Chart the most *direct* path to your goals—***Plan A***. No, you don't have to fill in *all* the boxes—they are a suggestion, not a requirement!

- For Plans B and C, add those jobs that might not be a direct path, *but which might ultimately lead you toward your goal* :

  - sales for product or software you know well? (in-house training, outside sales, demonstration team for trade shows)

  - development? (new product support, testing new products)

  - freelance? (clients you have gathered during your informational interviews)

  - part time? (getting your foot in the door while you work another job to help out with expenses—a local TV station requires all new hires to be the receptionist for 3 months)

  - closely related field? (teaching code, Web development)

  - contract? (short-term production such as ink and painter, texture mapping)

  - work abroad? (sales teams, software demonstration, in-house training)

Art, like morality, consists in drawing the line somewhere.
—*G.K. Chesterton*

- alternative paths? (pro bono work for causes you support—posters, sets, Website maintenance for organizations in the non-profit sector)

- sales in supplies for your industry? (paper sales, plastics, colorants)

- other options? *Plans B, C, D, or even E?*

Plan A	Plan B	Plan C

Plot the most *direct* path to your goals — **Plan A.**

Add those jobs which might not be a direct path, *but which might ultimately lead you toward your goal* (Plans B and C). You can see that the paths for Plan B and C are not straight, but contribute toward your ultimate goal. Explore many options, remembering to enjoy the quality of the journey.

See Sample Job Map on the next page.

Can't stand to fill in boxes? *Draw your own map* with viable options for Plans A, B, and C.

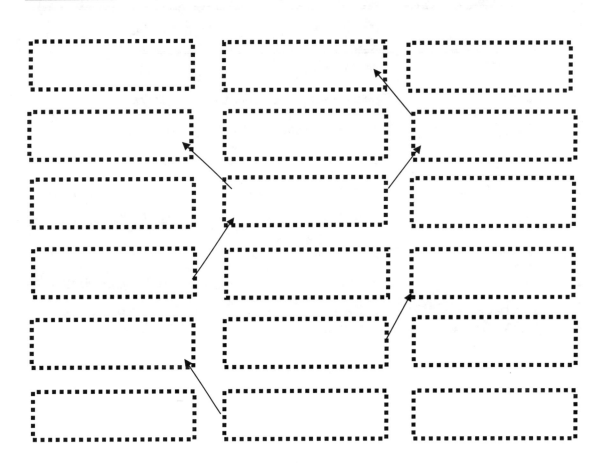

Plan A	Plan B	Plan C
Partner	Sole Ownership	Educator
Account Executive	Freelance Account Coordinator	Gallery Owner
Executive Producer	Freelance Executive Producer	Web Gallery Owner
Producer	Freelance Producer	Art Representative
Creative Director	Freelance Ass't Producer	Retail Art Sales/Framing
Art Director	Software Sales Manager	Teach Drawing/Parks & Rec
Graphic Designer Web Designer Animator	Freelance Graphic Design Freelance Web Design Freelance Animator	Enter Competitions Web-site Maintenance Freelance Comic Book Art
Ass't Designer Ass't Web Designer Ass't Animator	Software Sales Test Software Game Tester	Sales at Print House Counter at Print House Night Shift at Print House
Production Artist Ink and Painter	Software Demonstration Game Demonstration	Local Band Posters Teach Computer Literacy
	Keep part-time job as waitstaff	Keep retail sales job and freelance

A happy person is not a person in a certain set of circumstances, but rather a person with a certain set of attitudes. —Hugh Downs

Networking

All through your business life, you'll be *networking*. **Networking is the "buzzword" for *who you know*.**

You'll want to expand your acquaintances because people tend to hire professionals they know and can trust.

Freelance opportunities and hiring are done with people who've met face to face.

- This can mean those you've met at professional organizational meetings, but also it can mean the people you play softball with or the people you meet at the gym or your high school classmates or your Uncle Bobby Joe or Tia Margarita.

Your goal in networking is ***expanding who you know in business.*** Business contacts are personal, but business relationships are **not** personal.

- That sounds contradictory, doesn't it?

- Another way to say that is: you tend to hire, consult, work with those whom who you know, **but** what is *done to* people in the name of *business* is not considered personal because what is done is for *the best of the business, not necessarily the people involved.*

- For example, you've gotten a contract to construct a Website for a business, but you cannot do all the work yourself. You hire friends you know can help you do the job. (Here is the personal contact.) The client, however, has run out of funding and eliminates all but a minimal Website. Your friend's position is now redundant and you have to let him/her go. What you are doing now is not based on your personal relationship, but on your professional or business relationship.

- That said, however, it should be noted that the best businesses nurture *both* the business *and* the people involved, since *a contented, satisfied* (emotionally, intellectually, physically, and spiritually) *worker is the most productive.*

In **networking,** your goal is to *get to know others* in your field who are already working in the field. Through your networking, you may be fortunate enough to find:

- a mentor, someone who will guide your early career;

- you will find those who need your services, whether on contract, freelance, or a permanent basis;

- you will find information which might aid you in your job search, such as tips on: who to talk to; what to do about financial matters or needless expenses; what and whom to avoid; where to concentrate your search for clients or employment.

Every time you make a phone call or e-mail for a Lead I, you are **networking.** You are establishing a contact.

- *This function remains the same whether you are employed (or seeking employment), freelancing, contracting, or prospecting for clients.*

- You are a business asset to the person you contact because you are highly trained and eager to work, and the person you contact is *your* asset because of their established position and experience.

Your business contacts are like a garden to be carefully tended. One place that is particularly fertile for networking is your professional association, such as AIA (American Institute of Architects), ASID (American Society of Interior Designers), IDSA (Industrial Design Society of America), AIGA (American Institute of Graphic Arts), among many others.

- A national list of arts and design related professional organizations can be found in the Addenda of this book.

- Highlight an organization that would suit your professional education and visit the Website for information on your local chapter.

- Student memberships are *always* less expensive than professional ones, so take advantage of your student status to start meeting professionals soon. How about a professional membership as a graduation present?

- **Note**: Most professional organizations charge an at-the-door fee to offset speaker costs. You do not have to be a member to go to these meetings, but your at-the-door cost may be higher (for instance, $10 rather than $5). *Is it worth it to go to meetings where professionals are hiring? That's a no-brainer.*

It's all right to have butterflies in your stomach. Just get them to fly information. —Rob Gilbert

Your professional organization is a group of professionals working in your field who meet to discuss, plan, support and promote the industry.

- It will have regular meetings, which are part social and part business.

- It will be a place where you will meet professionals, arrange possible internships or assistantships, and start friendships with like-minded people.

- It will have group rates (which are much cheaper than individual rates) on insurance of various sorts (life, health, injury, inability to work, fire, property, among others). In some states, individual insurance policies are all but impossible to obtain.

- It will be productive for you (your corporation) professionally, socially, and financially.

Here are some **networking tips** for any grad:

1. Develop a *networking* plan

    a. What association should you belong to?

    b. When does it meet? (Arrange for time to go to the meeting.)

    c. Take some business cards to exchange (keep the ones you get in exchange for a Lead I and make them part of your database of acquaintenances).

    d. Shake hands firmly (not a crushing grip, but not a dead fish, either).

    e. Look people in the eye.

    f. Introduce yourself—first and last name. Remember, you're stepping into the professional ranks now. (Use the 10-second version of your TMAY—See *Interview* section of this book.)

g. Prepare your 3 favorite open-ended questions to be used as conversation starters

h. ***Be more interested in others than you are in yourself***—it's one of the tricks to overcome shyness.

2. Set a goal to **make at least 1 networking call a week** (informational interview—Lead I).

3. **Develop a good system** to organize the business cards you receive, especially the ones from your networking situations.

    a. There are card files and slip sheets made especially for business cards.

    b. Make a note about your conversation and date of meeting, so you can use these contacts to get feedback on your portfolio and to invite them to your portfolio show at graduation.

4. Develop a mailing list from your network. Regularly (once every couple of months) mail (or e-mail) these people something of interest.

5. Every six months, contact people on your *secondary* networking list.

    a. Your *primary* list contains those contacts who've responded positively, been helpful, have used your work, or are the most promising leads.

    b. ***Ask how you may be of service***, *rather than asking for their business or to be hired.*

6. At ***networking*** events, introduce as many people to each other as you can.

The method of the enterprising is to plan with audacity and execute with vigor. —Christian Bovee

73

7. **Respect** the time of those who you call. Make the connection brief, to the point, and of value to the other person.

8. **Thank *everyone* who gives you a lead** or needed information.

   a. Thank them verbally.

   b. Send them a note or e-mail.

   c. Why not use a color copy, scanned drawing, or digital photo of your work on the back of a post card or on your letterhead?

   d. Thank people even if the contact does not lead to a business deal. It may lead to business later!

9. **Be consistent** in your attendance of professional meetings. Showing up is the first step to success!

   a. You must attend events regularly and become known to people if you are to be a successful networker. Don't expect to go to events every few months and have it pay off.

   b. **Volunteer** for a committee or work party. You'll meet lots of people who have done the same and you could just meet someone who will lead you to a job, client, or gig!

10. When you see people you've met, offer your hand to shake **and** offer your name once again.

    ▪ You might say, "*Hi Bill, I'm Jamie McCall. We met at the Design Conference last summer.*"

11. **Take the initiative**. The success of *your* corporation depends on **you**.

12. Ask the person you're talking to what s/he would do in your shoes. You'll get some useful information and great help. **Thank them!**

13. Have fun! ***Your attitude is completely in your control.*** Consider this recreational and you *will* have fun.

Note: If you are an established professional in your field, professional associations are of immense value as well, for the reasons stated above, and to meet younger entries in the marketplace. This is the place to meet hot new talent. They'll never be cheaper!

Many disciplines are computer oriented and supported today, and since these industries are youth oriented, the youth you meet at a professional organization might be the person to hire you tomorrow—even if s/he looks like your son or daughter.

"Say, did you say you needed a designer? I talked to one just the other day. I know I've got that follow-up letter in here somewhere."

Leads are business contacts made through personal meetings, phone calls, e-mail, Website visits, and published media.

Leads are *possible* clients, employers, or employees. Leads "lead" you to jobs and to clients through *personal contacts*; your availability and capabilities are passed around in conversations. That your name is passed around is every reason to make your business contacts *as professional and pleasant as possible.*

Leads are an extension of networking. You'll be

- extending your business acquaintances;

- gathering information about your industry;

- researching companies which fit your own goals, values, and ideals—a place where you fit, and which fits you;

- asking for advice;

- inquiring as to how others have gotten a start in your industry;

- by making a phone call, e-mail, or fax to those in your industry (Lead I);

- researching;

- using libraries, the Internet, and published resources to gather information about companies, clients, and directions in your industry.

These leads will be the beginning of your own network and the foundation of a database of possible employers, employees, and clients. Preparation for the phone calls is a **must**—see the following section. Finally, note on the Lead Chart on page 93 where the best leads come from so you can mine this resource.

Lead Is are Informational Interviews. That means that you e-mail or call working professionals to find out how they got started in your profession.

You do not ask for a job or an internship, but by expressing your interest, you allow the contact the opportunity to offer you a start in the business by taking their time to answer your questions and becoming interested in you.

Informational Interviews offer several opportunities for your corporation:

- You learn how to talk to other business people in a non-threatening atmosphere (over the phone).

- You learn up-to-the-minute market information.

- You learn the inside stories of those who are in your business which will provide help for your own career.

- You gain valuable contacts.

Preparation for informational interviews:

- From your resource list, select a magazine or book to find current information on a working professional in your field.

- Look up
    1. what kind of work they do
    2. who their clients are
    3. where they work
    4. revenues
    5. how many people work for them, and
    6. how long they've been in business.

When you're through changing, you're through. —Bruce Barton

While some of this information might not be available, most will be! Go through the Interview Scenario which follows to ask for some time to speak. You'll have prepared some *open-ended* questions to ask when you call. Ask your prepared questions. Thank him/her politely. Send him/her a thank you note.

At first this will be difficult, but there is **so much** current information to be gained, and **so much** benefit in terms of business maturity to be gained, that it is worth the momentary twinges of panic. Believe it or not, some students even consider this fun! (Go figure!)

Note: If you've decided to make a phone call for an informational interview, **call during business hours** (Monday–Friday, 8 A.M.–5 P.M.).

While it is important for you to learn to talk to people you don't know over the phone (you'll have to do it lots during your working lifetime), **e-mail** is also a viable alternative. (*Resources for e-mail addresses in Where do you find information for Leads in the Addenda of this book.*)

With deadlines, creative professionals do not always have time to talk on the phone, but can respond to e-mail while on the road, on a break, or after working hours.

Here are some tips:

- Ask just 3 questions in a Lead I e-mail. A list of good questions follows on page 81.

- Send out at least 3 times (or more) as many e-mails as you need—a response rate of 30% is *fabulous*! 10% is more typical.

- **Do not group e-mail**. Cut and paste your message into each individual e-mail. If *you* received a group e-mail asking for a response, would **you** take the time to respond to it? Probably not.

- When you receive a response, **send another e-mail of thanks**. (Don't hit reply—it takes too much time to download after several replies.) Just a one-line thanks will do—always thank the respondent *for the time* s/he's taken. (In business, of course, time is money.)

   Hint: Prepare for several Lead Ones at once, so if one doesn't respond favorably, you have another to pursue.

Lead I or **Informational Interview** questions should be *open-ended*—answered with more than a one- or two-word answer.

- Find good questions that open great conversations. Save those to use again in the list below. The best are often those asking for advice. Most people are delighted to talk about themselves and give out advice.

- Do not be afraid that you are invading someone's privacy when calling or e-mailing. That person can always say s/he doesn't have time, or ignore your e-mail. What have you lost by asking? **Don't worry. Get started!**

- Decide on something you like to do—play video games? call your friends? watch television?—and *don't allow yourself to do that* **until** you've done your Informational Interview for the week.

- **YOU MUST PREPARE** what you're going to say on the phone ***before you call***, (just in case you're like the rest of us and your brains dribble out your ears into a puddle on the floor when you're scared). **Never "wing it." Preparation is rewarded with respect.**

Here are some open-ended questions to start your Lead Is (Informational Interviews).

1. How did *you* get started?

2. What are your recommendations for a student about to graduate?

3. What computer programs do you consider important to work with your firm? Are they changing?

4. What do you expect from people who have graduated from a _____ (program) in _____?

5. What do you look for in an employee?

6. Do you use interns? freelance? part-time? contract? full-time employees?

7. Could you describe the atmosphere in your company? (or, Could you describe a typical day in your company?)

8. What associations/organizations or groups would you recommend that I join?

9. What skills/education do you recommend?

10. Where do you see your industry going in the next 3 – 5 years?

11. Can you think of anyone else I should be talking to?

12. List below other good questions you've found that open up a conversation:

Every human being on this earth is born with a tragedy, and it isn't original sin. He's born with the tragedy that he has to grow up. A lot of people don't have the courage to do it. —Helen Hayes

A sample conversation might go like this:

"MICROBITS ENTERPRISES" (a pleasant voice answers the phone).

You say:
Hello, may I speak with _____? the personnel director **or** name of the contact person in your research (art director? animator? producer?)

Your contact answers: *Bill Brammer, Design*

You say:
Hello, my name is _____.

a) *I'm graduating from the _____in _____ (month) in _____ (department).*

OR

(b) *I am gathering information for (a class at _____) or (your corporation).*

You say:
Do you have a moment to speak with me?

If the contact answers NO,

You ask: *When would be a good time to call?*

OR

You ask: *Is there anyone who might be free to answer some questions?*

If the answer is still negative, *thank* the person and hang up.

Do not react with anything other than politeness.

If the contact answers YES:

You say*:*
> *May I ask you a few questions about your company and how you got started? It will only take a few minutes.*

Now, **you ask the questions you have prepared** for this call.

- Ask slowly and politely.

- Always ask, "Is there is anyone else you should be talking to?" This is a marketing tactic, asking for the next lead—polite, non-intrusive, but knowledgeable about marketing.

You say:
> *Thank you very much for taking the time to talk with me, Mr./Ms. _____.*

Your contact says:
> *You're welcome. Bring your portfolio by when you're ready.*

- Should you take your portfolio by for feedback when it's ready? **Yes!** A door has opened. You march through it with confidence. You might just meet some really cool people!

You say:
> *Thank you, I will. Good-bye.* Hang up.

If you feel comfortable *writing* a thank you letter, do so, but you must follow up in some way.

- A handwritten note will be fine—put it on a post card with your art work on the other side—but a more business-like way is to write a short business letter (see sections on Cover Letters and Thank You Letters).

- *E-mail is OK ,too.*

- After all, **someone has taken a chunk of *his/her* day to help *you* out. *Consideration is memorable*!**

Now you can play games on the Internet for an hour! Have fun!

Informational Interviews are conversations with professionals in your field to get current information about the marketplace so that you can appropriately direct your career. This type of lead requires a personal contact by phone, e-mail, or face-to-face conversation.

By personal meeting, phone, fax, or e-mail

- Fill in as much information as you can obtain on the Lead I worksheets, using Leads Resources, Print, and Web in the Addenda of this book. This will be the start of your database of potential jobs, clients, and customers.

- Do *one Informational Interview per week during your educational program*, and ***one a day after graduation***.

Copy this information onto your database or keep a file for your e-mails and calls.

Lead I

- Name of company: _____

- Complete address: _____

- Web address: _____

- Phone: _____E-mail:_____

- Contact person: Mr./Ms. _____
  (confirm spelling while you are on the phone)

- Title: _____

- Type of work done by company: _____

- Major Clients are: 1. _____
  2. _____
  3. _____

- What does the company's work look/sound like? (tape a sample on the back if possible) _____

- How many people work in this company? _____

- How long has it been in business? _____

- Is this company or industry expanding (will there be room for *you*)? Ask! __

- (a) 4 *open-ended* questions you've prepared to ask this contact/lead?
- (b) 4 answers.

1. (a) _____

    (b) _____
    _____
    _____

2. (a) _____

    (b) _____
    _____
    _____

3. (a) _____

    (b) _____
    _____
    _____

It's what you do after you know it all that counts. —John Wooden

4. (a) Is there anyone else I should be talking to?

(b)_____
_____
_____

- Possibilities: Freelance? _____ Internship? _____ Part-time? _____
  Contract? _____ Full-time? _____

- Lead came from _____
  (If this is a person, be sure to *follow up by sending them a thank you note*.)
  Remember, this is networking.

  Thank you sent _____

- Follow-up notes:

Lead IIs are research-only leads. They are the beginning of your job and client database. You are collecting names and contact numbers of people and companies you'd like to work for or work with, or even possibly employ.

Keep these on file, in a list, in photo-copies of indices, on a database, or in your business card file (yet another reason to go to those professional associations).

When you are ready to graduate, you'll know where you fit in the marketplace, and where you want to focus. *You'll be in charge* of your own fate instead of blowing around like a seed in the wind, hoping against hope you'll land in the right place.

Fill in the **Lead Chart** that follows as you progress through the leads to determine your best sources of information.

After you graduate, your leads will be a **gold mine** of client/employer/employee information. Then, make a *full-time job* of your job search. Make 5 contact/lead calls a day until you find the **right place for you** as a representative of your corporation.

Note: It is typical after graduation that you'll experience a little emotional dip — someone or something (your instructors and your educational program) has been demanding things of you for some years, so you've been *outer directed*. **Now** you have to be *inner directed* rather than *outer directed*, and that can cause some confusion after graduation. Some people feel cut adrift. You'll develop a plan to get through it, and follow through with that plan.

If your Lead Is and networking efforts have lead to a job directly after graduation, congratulations! *But, if not, hang in there!* Continue with Lead Is, with your networking efforts, remembering you are acting on behalf of your own corporate entity, one that has trained for success.

Genius is the gold in the mine; talent is the miner who works and brings it out. —Lady Blessington

- Just a reminder—it typically takes 8 to 23 weeks to find a job, even longer in a recession.

    o That's why it's important to get a running start while you're in school *or while you have a job*. (No job hunting on your employer's time, however— grounds for instant dismissal!)

    o One more reminder—your student loans require repayment installments beginning 6 months from graduation. *Get going!*

Lead II

A Lead II is a research lead. As Lead IIs accumulate, they become the basis of your database for possible contacts, employers, clients, and customers.

- **Complete** the worksheets with as much information as possible.

    o Do two Lead IIs per week during your educational program and 2 per day after graduation.

    o These are companies you'd like to work for, to contract with, or possibly hire for your own contract work.

    o Use resources from the Resource List in the Addenda.
    My favorite? *ID (International Design)* magazine's December issue each year is a sourcebook of designers and suppliers in several disciplines.

- **Copy this blank to your database.**

Few things help an individual more than to place responsibility on him, and to let him know that you trust him. —Booker T. Washington

Lead II

- Name of company: _____

- Complete address: _____

- Web address: _____

- Phone: _____ E-mail:_____

- Contact person: Mr./Ms._____

- Title: _____
    Designer, Director of Human Resources, Art Director?
    Get the spelling right. Confirm by phone.

- Type of work done by this company:_____

- Clients are:
    1. _____
    2. _____
    3. _____

- What does the company's work look/sound like? (find a sample to attach to this form) _____

- How many people work for this company? _____

- How long has it been in business? _____

- Is this company or industry expanding (is there room *for you*)? Ask! _____

- Possibilities: Freelance? _____ Intern? _____ Part-time? _____

- Contract? _____ Full-time? _____

- Lead came from? _____

- *Thank you note* sent for lead (if necessary)? _____

- Follow-up notes:

> ### Lead Chart

- Sometimes you get a chance to talk to one of your Lead IIs—it then becomes a Lead I and you replace it with another Lead II. Your goal, after all, is to expand the network of people you know. Once this system is learned, you'll employ it all your working lifetime. Why wouldn't you keep track of the people you've met with whom you'd enjoy working?

- **Fill in the chart** to determine where the best leads come from. Use that information to keep mining the best resource.

Company Name	Source? (Web, personal lead, book of lists, yearbook, phonebook, magazine, other?)

1.

2.

3.

4.

5.

6.

7.

8.

9.

10.

11.

12.

13.

14.

15.

16.

17.

18.

19.

20.

Miracles are nothing more than ordinary events that lie outside your current structure of knowing.
—Maria North

_____Thank you note or e-mail sent for personal referral?

Graphic Presentation: Marketing Documents

This segment contains the paperwork you and your corporation present to the public, including

- résumés (one for the trade, one faxable, and one in digital format),

- a cover letter,

- a thank you letter,

- a references sheet,

- a Sample Sheet, and

- a business card.

These are **marketing tools**, *sales documents* to sell what you (the corporation) can do, not only verbally, but *visually*. If you are in a design field, think of these documents as portfolio pieces. In addition, you should acquire at least *2 current letters of recommendation.*

You should be approaching this graphic presentation not only as a vehicle for conveying clear information, but as a **design *tour de force.***

The Résumé

A résumé is a list of your skills, accomplishments, and job history. When an employer or client reads it, s/he should clearly and easily understand **what you can do. A résumé is also the platform from which you will launch your corporate marketing, and it will reflect your design skills and attention to detail.** It is the foundation of your interviewing subject matter, so make sure it reflects your strengths and capabilities so that you can use these during the interview.

Readability and Scanning

- It is important that a *human reader* can scan your résumé in 10 –15 seconds, so the use of various letterform weights (bolds, italics, underlines, etc.) can be employed to lead the eye down the page and to accent important keywords.

- If your résumé is to be *digitally scanned* before a human being reads it, then keywords need to be included at the top of your résumé.

Keywords

- **What are keywords?** These words can be found in the *job descriptions* and *qualifications needed* on many joblines, and on job posting boards on the Internet, such as the *Monster Board* at *Monster.com*. What category should you look under? The job title you will be applying for: assistant graphic designer, drafter, ink and painter, etc.

- It is important that you include keywords describing your skills in 4 categories (*personal, digital, conceptual, traditional*) in the *first 15 lines* of your résumé that describe the qualifications required by the job you're interested in.

  However! You should use only the keywords that really describe your capabilities, so if you cannot work on a team, do not put the keywords *team player* on your résumé. If you cannot describe a time when you've employed a particular skill or cannot prove your skill at a software program, do not use those keywords on your résumé.

A *résumé* always has three sections: skills, education, and experience. It can have at least two more optional sections: Objective (or Qualifications Summary) and Honors and Awards (or Professional Associations).

The ***order** in which you present these parts* represents *what you're trying to market.*

- Just finished an educational program? Put your skills first, followed by education.

- Had 20 years' experience in your field? Put your experience first, followed by education.

- Had 20 years' experience in a field not represented by your education? Put experience first, skills second, and education last.

- If your sales and marketing approach emphasizes your experience and you want to place that section first on your résumé, you will want to place a Keyword Summary (or Qualifications Summary) as the *first* category on your résumé to satisfy that digital scanner.

1. Skills

- Place in a four column set-up across the page or in some other organizational format that is *easy to read*.

- You will typically have three or four *groupings of skills* (group similar skills for easy reading). The order in which you present these is your own choice:

    - **Personal**   - **Traditional**   - **Digital**   - **Conceptual**

a. **Personal**—those personal skills that define your strengths, choose 6 – 8 that most typify your personal skills, such as

- dependable
- leadership
- good listening skills
- persuasiveness
- maturity
- sensitivity
- adaptability
- competitive
- pragmatic
- self-starter
- self-motivated
- friendly
- good follow-up
- process-oriented
- willingness to work hard
- communication skills
- flexible
- enthusiastic
- team player
- confidence
- common sense
- troubleshooting
- idealism
- empathy
- patient
- speaking skill
- independent
- energy
- customer service
- sincerity
- ability to relocate
- attention to detail
- work until job is done
- entrepreneurial spirit
- team builder
- goal-oriented

b. **Traditional**—those skills which **predate computers,** such as

- sketching
- drafting
- sculpture
- drum micing
- airbrush
- scratch board
- rendering
- large format cameras
- metalwork
- modelmaking
- cartooning
- acrylics

c. Digital—hardware and platforms; **all** the software you know (plus the version you've worked with if it is pertinent). *Many résumés are scanned for software programs*, so be sure you have included *all* you have   experience with.

You may want to star those you are proficient in (as opposed to familiar with), placing a key at the bottom of the résumé or the section. *Learn keystrokes –* they save about 1 hour of productivity per day; you may be tested.

Spelling of programs **must be correct.** Check *corporate Websites* for proper spelling of software programs. *Example*: <u>*Adobe.com*</u>

Some current popular programs are:

Adobe Illustrator®	Kinetix 3D Studio MAX®
Adobe PageMaker®	Lightscape LVS®
Adobe Photoshop®	Lightwave®
Aldus Freehand®	LINGO®
Alias PowerAnimator®	Lotus 1-2-3®
AutoCAD®	Macromedia FreeHand Graphics®
Autodesk (Kinetix) 3D Studio Max®	Macromedia Director®
Autodesk Animator®	MS Excel®
C++®	MS Office®
ClarisWorks®	MS PowerPoint®
CorelDRAW!®	MS Word®
Corel WordPerfect®	MS Works®
Flash®	QuarkXPress®
Fractal Design Painter®	Softimage or SOFTIMAGE®
HTML	Softimage TOONZ®

Others you use

_____

_____

d. Conceptual—areas of study or knowledge

This might include seminars you've taken, updates to your skills, student project areas you've mastered, or classes you've taken.

- 3-D modeling
- Publication design
- Collateral design
- Color and materials
- Patternmaking
- Hospitality design
- Dance notation
- Animated prosthetics
- Art direction
- Storyboarding
- Project management

- Identity development
- Typography
- Theatrical effects
- Textiles
- Print production
- Signage design
- Kitchen and bath
- Concept drawing
- Scripting
- Marketing
- Music theory

2. Education

Your schools and educational background are offered in *reverse chronological order.*

Check the degree designator for your program. Some common degrees:
- AA - AAA - BA - BS - BFA - MA - MFA

Should you use periods between letters? *Your choice;* traditional résumés do. Many contemporary résumés do not.

Should you spell out your degree? *Your choice.* Associate of Arts? Associate of Applied Arts? Bachelor of Arts? Bachelor of Science? Bachelor of Fine Arts? Master of Arts? Master of Fine Arts?

List city and state for your high school diploma as well as the name of the high school. **Wolfpack High School, Claremont, CA**

If you are over 30 years old, it is not necessary to list your high school graduation, your high school honors, or your high school recommendations.

3. Experience

The jobs you've held should be offered in *reverse chronological order.* There should be *two groups* **if you have had any industry experience** (student studio or volunteer or internship):

    a. **Industry Related** and
    b. **Other**

If you have had no industry experience, place your experience all together in reverse chronological order. ***If you have no industry experience, now*** is the time to arrange for some referrals for volunteer work or **internships** (even if they are only 5 hours a week) to gain some experience.

Your experience should be described with *action words*: implemented, trained, oversaw, designed, etc. See ***Active Verbs for Résumés***, which follows.

Include **all** your experience. You may decide not to include jobs during high school, etc. but omissions are considered as much a falsehood as inflating your experience. Either are grounds for instant dismissal. Be especially careful on your employment application. To be on the safe side, make a list of all the jobs you've had and carry a copy to supply if asked. Print it on your letterhead, of course.

If you are mature, and have had lots of jobs that are not relevant to your new career, consider having a separate sheet which lists those jobs under categories of type of job, like a *functional résumé (see paragraphs that follow in this section on Functional Résumés)*.

If you have *not had any jobs which relate to your new degree*, put in the experience that you *have* had, including fast-food, etc. These are *marketable skills*. What you are demonstrating is:

- that you know how to show up for work,
- that you can work on a team,
- that you can prioritize,
- that you have customer service skills,
- that you can be responsible for cash, and
- that you can work quickly and efficiently.

All your skills are marketable skills! Remember, **a résumé is a sales and marketing document**.

Format for detailing your experience

The ***position*** is mentioned first, and then the company and city where it is located. Dates of employment should be mentioned, and can be shown before or after the listing.

Caution! ***Do not*** use the résumé for reference names and phone numbers. This is very unprofessional and a rookie error. We will construct a separate *References* sheet to include these.

Category for Objectives

- *Should be included* on your résumé *if* **you are answering an advertisement or a posting on a jobline** that mentions a specific job title, such as *assistant designer*.

- **If, however, your objective is generic**, what an objective really says is that you are inexperienced at marketing yourself: *I want an entry level job in the field that I love.* This type of objective states the obvious, takes up space, and **shouts of inexperience**. Is that the impression that you want an employer to get from your marketing documents?

- **An objective can be limiting.** For instance, you may ultimately want to be an Art Director, and if you state this in your objective, you will probably *only be considered* for the position of Art Director, for which you are not yet qualified (lack of experience). You'd risk being overlooked for a lower level job, for which you are exactly suited.

- **If you are retraining** and your experience does not support the job you seek (but your education does), *you may want to include a **broad** objective* so that the reviewer knows what job you're applying for since cover letters, which would explain the situation, often get separated from the résumé.

- You may want to replace "Objectives" with a "Summary" which reads like your mission statement, stuffed full of keywords.

Honors, Awards, Hobbies, Interests, and Professional Associations can each be included as a separate category after experience.

- Refrain from mentioning specific religious or political organizations to avoid discrimination (use "edited church sponsored newsletter" or "organized school political group," etc.)

Do not **include marital status, number of dependents, or health information**. While this used to be a part of résumés, personal information is no longer included, due to Equal Opportunity legislation.

Complete your résumé by offering ***References and Portfolio Available Upon Request*** at the bottom. You can use a footer for this. There is new thought that it is *a given* that references are available and that if you are in an artistic profession, that you'll have a portfolio or demo tape/CD.

- Do you need some *visual completion* of the page itself—something to keep the type from falling off the page? Use the "References…" line (or split your letterhead to put your name at the top and address and contact numbers at the bottom). If not, perhaps you can use the space to keep your résumé on one page. Here again, you have a choice.

Format—There are three typical formats for résumés.

1. ***Chronological***: lists jobs in *reverse* chronological order.

   - *Focuses on experience* at specific places. The experience section of the résumé is dominant, and skills and application of skills are clearly outlined. This is a traditional format and has been used for about 90% of résumés written.

2. ***Functional***: lists and describes qualifications in depth.

   - *The focus is on a specific job type and the many companies in which you displayed the skills needed for this type of job.* Jobs are listed *after descriptive paragraphs* about each skill in one line each by company and date only, with no elaboration.

   - Example:
     Sales representative. Developed a sales clientele and managed a sales book for select customers for moderate women's fashion retailer. Excelled at customer service. Keyholder. Elevated to management at each store.
     20__ – 20__ Kangaroos & Koalas, Chicago, IL
     1997 – 2000 Salina's, St. Louis, MO
     1994 – 1997 Baker and Bell Fashions, Pocatello, ID

3. **Combination**: *lists capabilities and skills as well as experience in jobs*.

  - The résumé on page 115 is a combination résumé, with a complete list of skills and relevant experience. Those finishing an educational program may find this the most useful.

Design

The résumé is a sales and marketing document. Construct it so that, as a *leave-behind*, it represents you, the corporation, and demonstrates why you are a valuable asset.

Your cover letter, thank you letter, résumé, and list of references should all be on the same letterhead, so that you have *unity of presentation* for your corporation.

The *type font should remain consistent* from document to document. Use a font size no smaller than comparable to 8 point in Times New Roman. 10 point comparable is optimum. A 12 point comparable can be a bit too large for the body but works well for your name.

Your documents should be viewed from a design perspective as well as a format and grammatical perspective. Remember, you are representing yourself as a creative person. How will you present your corporate approach to creativity?

Think marketing. *Think marketing.* **Think marketing.** Tailor your approach and résumé for your target audience. You may have several résumés framed for particular targets in mind.

  - one, black and white, very traditional targeted toward a conservative client;

  - one very colorful with scans of your portfolio up the side for art directors or dot-coms; and

- one in a non-traditional format—pop-up? collaged? in a pizza box? Your imagination and budget are the only limitations.

Caution! Take care not to pare this document down so far in the name of "clean design" that it does not sell your skills, education and experience. *You can go "over the top" in spareness as well as wordiness.* Remember that **the résumé is a marketing document**.

After you've constructed your document, pin it up on the wall as you would a design problem.

- Does it have impact?
- Is it centered with similar margins top and bottom?
- What draws your attention?
- Where are the focal points? Do they work for readability?
- Do the **bolds** lead you from stopping point to stopping point?
- Have you utilized white space well?
- How do the groups of text (grid units) look in terms of positive and negative space ?

Papers

You should have *a résumé printed on good looking medium weight paper* to be distributed to the trade and other interested parties, during interviews and during portfolio review. Coverstock and cardstock are too heavy for résumés. Check the watermark to make sure it is right side up. (Good designers check *all* the details.)

AND AND AND AND AND AND!

You should have *a résumé printed on white paper in black ink*, which can be *faxed* clean. No half-tones (grays) should be used, as many fax machines are still working on Xerox technology (instead of printer technology), and will only read either end of the value scale (black or white).

Note: If you want the well designed impact you've worked hard to achieve, *print out a copy of your résumé and take it to a fax machine.*

- Why? A résumé faxed *from a computer will not retain its format*, but *may print out on the receiving end on two or three pages.*

Size—*one* readable page

Unless you have several years' experience in the field—then, of course, yours will be longer. You can submit a page of supplemental information, such as seminars attended or additional training or non-related experience, on a separate page, on your letterhead.

You may want a one-page résumé and a one-page VITA of CREDITS (list of professional accomplishments)—see following pages.

Use the **8.5" x 11"** format in the US and the metric standard when abroad. Anything larger is annoying and will get tattered, and anything smaller will get fall out of a file and get lost.

Companies that deal with hundreds of résumés will probably digitally scan your résumé, looking for key words (often specific software program skills).

- **Warning!** Some companies ask for faxed résumés and run them through a scanner as they come in. If *keywords* are not encountered in the top 1/3 of the résumé, the résumé is shredded. If keywords are found, the résumé is placed in a pile for a human to read.

- *Research* to find out if key words are an issue: check the jobline at the company Website, and check *Monster.com* for industry keywords for the position you're applying for.

- In addition, some companies are asking for

  1. a sans serif font (Helvetica, Gill Sans, or Arial, for example)

  2. with no hard returns (hitting *Enter* or *Return* on the keyboard)

3. Tabs, spacing, and columns are good options in this format.

Older scanners do not read italics, shaded or shadowed graphics, nor do they read columned formats. Call to inquire about scanning hardware and software. A call to the jobline or a visit to the Website should determine if there is a specific format demanded for the first screening of candidates.

It is not uncommon for résumés to be e-mailed.

Since compatibility of software, hardware, and servers is often an issue in e-mail, a better option is placing your résumé on a Website and then referring to it in an e-mail message, phone mail, or phone conversation. Or, you can attach your résumé to an e-mail, include a scanned version as a *jpeg,* or include your URL as a link.

Privacy issues, security, and tampering, however, are some of the issues worth investigating in relation to Website postings. Without making gender an issue, a candidate may not want to reveal his/her personal address or phone number, for instance, opting instead for an answering service and post office box.

The use of common fonts such as Courier, Arial, Helvetica, or Times New Roman can help with transmission and receipt of an e-mailed résumé—but are no guarantee that it will arrive in text, rather than symbols. Text files have this common difficulty, although much has been done recently to overcome this deficiency.

Note: Some interviewers will not take the time to visit a Website. (Imagine that you have 50 résumés to review, 25 of them with Website references. Would *you* take the time to visit them all?) If you *do* have a Website, make sure yours is secure so that you are sure you are representing yourself with accurate information.

Digital Résumés

Job boards on the Internet often require a digital résumé. For creatives, this is difficult to construct, as you're used to using visual-spatial skills on your résumé to set you apart from the next candidate. How can you create a digital résumé? See the next section for specifications.

The Wow Factor

Overnight courier/delivery systems still have their advantages if the package, seen and experienced as a whole, is of prime importance. Opening your graphic presentation package should be a visual delight in itself.

There may be no errors. *None.* No spacing problems, no misspellings of computer programs, no typos, no spelling or grammatical errors, no printer problems.

- *Spell check*
- Proof-read for all of the above.
- Read it backwards so errors will show up.
- Ask someone to proofread for you to get an objective opinion.
- **No Errors!**

*An excellent resource: *Résumés for Dummies* by Joyce Lain Kennedy. See Resource List included in the Addenda.

```
┌ ▪ ▪ ▪ ▪ ▪ ▪ ▪ ▪ ▪ ▪ ▪ ▪ ▪ ▪ ▪ ┐
▪                               ▪
    Digital Résumé
▪                               ▪
└ ▪ ▪ ▪ ▪ ▪ ▪ ▪ ▪ ▪ ▪ ▪ ▪ ▪ ▪ ▪ ┘
```

You already have several résumés on disk to target different audiences — a more conservative one for conservative firms in black and white, a color and image résumé for the more design-oriented firm.

You may be asked to e-mail a résumé, and while some firms may open a file attachment with your well designed résumé, many will not because of digital viruses embedded in attachments. So, we'll construct an e-mail résumé that eliminates those risks and yet still serves as a marketing document.

As we've discussed earlier, your résumé is the foundation of your interview, your portfolio, and your marketing documents (cover letter, list of references, Sample Sheet, business card, etc.). All should have the same "look." The "look" sells your visual/spatial skills as well as the others you have listed in the top of your résumé.

The Wow Factor

> **A digital résumé is one that is a *text-only* document**, and those visual/spatial skills that you rely on to demonstrate your creativity are *not* available to you to the degree that they are in traditional résumés.
>
> So, how do you make your digital résumé have a "wow" factor? How about these?
>
> - Use a quote that sums you up (be sure to credit the originator, writer, singer, etc.).
>
> - Create a "mission statement" for your corporation.
>
> - List your professional enthusiasms.
>
> **What to include**: as on your hard copy résumé
>
> - ***Skills keywords***: those skills you have listed on your résumé, including personal, digital, traditional, and conceptual.
>
> - ***Experience:*** as on your résumé including job descriptors in reverse chronological order.

- **_Education_**: your expected degree and others in reverse chronological order.

- **_Objective_**: only if it is to target a specific job or a job category, not a generic "want a job in my field."

- **_Honors_** or Associations.

What you can use:

- Dashes, asterisks
- Left justify, 1″ or 1.25″ margins
- A sans serif type: Arial, Gill Sans, Helvetica, Univers
- Font size: 10 or 12 point (Arial typical)
- Space bar

What you can't do:

- No bullets
- No **BOLD**
- No underlining
- _No italics_
- No center justify or right justify
- No horizontal or vertical lines
- No parentheses or brackets
- No varying fonts or font sizes
- No compressed type

Now what?

Save it as a word processing document. "Text only" or "text only with line breaks" (ASCII file). E-mail it to a prospective employer or a client or post it on the Web.

Post it on the Web at

- Monster.com: http:www.monster.com—Monster has become the 500 lb. gorilla in the field, gobbling up rivals.
- Advertising Age: http://adage.com/job_bank
- American Job Bank: http://ajb.dni.us/seeker
- Career Mosaic: http://www.careermosaic.com/
- HotJobs.com: http://hotjobs.com/htdocs/myhotjobs.html
- Job Options: http://joboptions.com/esp/plsql/espan_enter.espan_home

Security Issues

When you post your portfolio or résumé on the Web, you are revealing your location and contact numbers to the world. You may want to consider using a separate Web address for replies from Web postings to protect your privacy. You may want to *omit your street address* and *phone number* (or employ a message answering service and post office box specifically for this purpose).

Your Name —————————————————————————

Address ————————————————— **City, State, Zip** ———————————

Phone ————————————————— **E-mail** ———————————————

Objective ————————————————————————————

Skills   **Personal**   **Traditional**   **Digital**   **Conceptual**

—————————————————————————————————————

—————————————————————————————————————

—————————————————————————————————————

—————————————————————————————————————

—————————————————————————————————————

Education

—————————————————————————————————————

—————————————————————————————————————

—————————————————————————————————————

—————————————————————————————————————

—————————————————————————————————————

Experience

    Industry Related

—————————————————————————————————————

    Other

—————————————————————————————————————

—————————————————————————————————————

—————————————————————————————————————

Honors and Activities

—————————————————————————————————————

References and Portfolio Upon Request

Bring sketches for your résumé and this completed résumé with you to the computer, so when you begin to construct it, you have all the tools you need.

Sample Résumé

Note: size should be 8.5" x 11" in the US and typical metric dimensions abroad

Your name goes on this line
Your address goes here, city, state, zip
Phone, fax, message, e-mail address

Skills

Personal	Traditional	Digital	Conceptual
team player	drafting	MS Office®	Publication design
customer service	airbrush	Freehand®	Collateral design
self-motivated	water media	Photoshop®	Print production
goal oriented	cartooning	Softimage®	Theatrical effects
common sense	pen/ink	QuarkXPress®	Toy design

Education
BA, University of _____, expected June 20, 20_____
Major: Arts of Animation and Design

Experience

Industry Related — **(list your freelance, internship, etc. in reverse chronological order)**

2/97 to present — *Graphics Specialist*, **Typeworks 24 Hour,** Seattle, WA
Aided 200 customers per shift, consulted for graphic design on special jobs. Advanced from receptionist to sales.

1/01 — *brochure* illustration, **Joyce, Tabor, and Cook**, Anaheim, CA
Designed and arranged for printing for a production company

9/00 — *cartoon for brochure*, **Philmore and Peters**, Bellingham, NC
Designed an ink illustration with color overlays for company picnic.

Other — (list any other jobs you've had in reverse chronological order.)

1/94-1/97 — Floor Manager, Saltwater Café, Bayou Bulge, LA
Advanced to floor manager in 2.5 years from pantry cook through waitstaff. Oversaw waitstaff of 7–9 servers for an upscale 150-seat seafood restaurant. Implemented liaison plan for kitchen staff and waitstaff with management team.

Honors and Awards — **Dean's List, University of _____, 4 quarters, '01-'02**
Portfolio and References Upon Request

Any Student   2323 Street Address, City, State, Zip, Phone, E-mail

Skills
Traditional   Drawing, Drafting, Acrylics, Gouache, Airbrush, Rendering, Cartooning,
                   Sculpture, Typography, Scriptwriting, Analogue Recording

Digital   PC/MAC, Freehand®, Premiere®, QuarkXPress®, Avid®, Director®,
                   Photoshop®, Illustrator®, 3D Studio Max®, HTML, Flash®, MS Office®

Personal   Creative, Time Management, Self-starter, Organized, Team Player,
                   Team Builder, Flexible, Dependable, Good Client Relationships

Conceptual   Concept Development, Color Boards, Non-linear Editing, Store
                   Planning, Storyboarding, Editorial Illustration, Website Management

Education   BA, University of _____, Any City, State
                   Expected _____, 20____. Major: Multimedia

Experience   Industry Related
                   Illustration for Red Cross, Seattle, WA 2002
                   Designed and executed poster illustration for non-profit organization
                   through Student Studio, an honors class specializing in pro bono work

                   Rendering for Big Builders, Issaquah, WA, 2002
                   Executed rendering for local builders for display at open house

                   Website Design for MediaGroup, Seattle, WA 2001
                   Designed and applied a Website for a dot.com consulting firm

                   Collateral Design, The House Store, Bellevue, WA 2001
                   Designed collateral pieces to support an upscale retail store

                   Other
                   Lead Line cook, My Favorite Burger, Bainbridge Island, WA 9/00–present
                   Prep and cook 200 orders per shift. Most Valuable Employee
                   Award, 9/01.

Honors   Most Improved Artist Award, Fall 2000
                   Second Prize, Student Show, University of _____, 2001

Portfolio Available for Viewing at www.anystudent.com

Sample Layout:
2 Column

When you **describe the tasks** in any job you've had in the **Experience** section of your résumé, you should **use past or present tenses of active verbs** in verb phrases.

- **Active verbs tell what you can do, which, after all, is the point of a résumé!** Try to have about *four verb phrases* to describe each job you've had. Start with the verb, and then use the descriptors: *Developed 20 options for client approval.*

- **Your résumé should read**:

  Jun '96 – Jul '97 *Telephone Sales*, **Ticketmaster,** Seattle, WA
  Answered 200 phone calls per day, resulting in 80% sales. Completed statistical analysis of each shift. Trained 20 new sales associates. Received Top Sales Staff, Dec.'96, June '97.

- **It should NOT read:**

  Jun '96 – Jul '97 Telephone Sales, Ticketmaster, Seattle, WA
  Duties included: Phone sales, shift figures, new sales staff training. Top Sales Staff, Dec. '96.

- **The difference is:**
  o the use of active verbs describing what the *actual tasks* were in the job

  o the focus on action, taking a positive approach and responsibility for work on the job.

As an employer, I want to know what kind of tasks I can hand off to you that do not have to be taught or supervised. This should *not* be a treasure hunt with cleverly placed clues. I'll want to visually scan your résumé to find out if you will be of use in my company.

Carefully describing the tasks of your jobs requires some thought to really dissect what it is you do at work. Be careful of exaggeration here, and on the other hand, a too spare appearance.

- Some useful *action verbs* follow. **Highlight** those you think might be of use to you. Use them to describe and quantify the jobs you've held. Put the results on the fill-in-the-blanks résumé.

acted	adapted	addressed	administered
advised	allocated	analyzed	appraised
approved	arranged	arbitrated	arranged
assembled	assessed	assigned	assisted
attained	authored		
balanced	budgeted	built	
calculated	cataloged	chaired	clarified
coached	collected	communicated	compiled
computed	classified	consolidated	conceptualized
contracted	coordinated	corresponded	counseled
created	critiqued		
designed	developed	delegated	devised
demonstrated	diagnosed	directed	dispatched
drafted	drew		
edited	educated	enabled	encouraged
engineered	enlisted	established	examined
explained	executed	evaluated	expedited
extracted			
fabricated	facilitated	familiarized	fashioned
forecast	formulated	founded	
generated	guided		

identified	illustrated	implemented	improved
increased	influenced	initiated	interpreted
instructed	inspected	instituted	integrated
invented			

laid out	lectured	listed

maintained	managed	mapped	marketed
mediated	modeled	moderated	monitored
motivated			

negotiated

operated	optimized	organized	originated
overhauled	oversaw		

painted	performed	persuaded	planned
prioritized	processed	prepared	produced
projected	programmed	promoted	publicized
purchased			

recommended	reconciled	recorded	recruited
remodeled	rendered	repaired	represented
researched	retrieved	reviewed	revitalized

scanned	sculpted	set goals	screened
shaped	sketched	served	solved
spoke	scheduled	stimulated	strengthened
summarized	supervised	surveyed	

tabulated	taught	trained	translated

upgraded

wrote

Others you've thought of:

Your graphic presentation *represents you, the corporation, to the marketplace* when you are not present.

Your business card, your résumé, your Sample Sheet, as well as other documents are called *leave-behinds,* and go into separate places in a company:

- Your business card may go into a card file or card sheet, grouped with others who do similar kinds of work—illustration, for example—in a Producer's or Art Director's office (there may be several people who occupy this position in a company).

- Your résumé may be placed in the Human Resources Department for consideration for a full-time position.

- Your Sample Sheet may go into a file of work to consider for contract or freelance work.

Your letterhead, therefore, must be consistent from document to document. You may opt to change your graphic presentation from time to time, but consistency is a virtue here, and so when you change the entire package—résumé, Sample Sheet, business card, letterhead, list of references—all must have the same "look."

- Block in rough sketches of the *look* of your letterhead and résumé on this page —use the margins. No points for neatness! Do at least 5 thumbnail sketches to consider how it looks **graphically.**

- **Your résumé represents your design capabilities. Consider:**

  o positive/negative space (use of white space and grid units)
  o blocks of type as shape
  o locations of "bolds" (visual circulation)—do they lead the eye down the page?
  o space, texture, line
  o color

A piece of sculpture or a painting is never a finished work. Simultaneously it answers a question which has been asked, and asks a new question.
—Robert Engman

- Remember, this represents *your corporation,* and is **often the first look someone gets of your work.**

- Now, sketch out your own résumé, as if it were a design problem.
  Use the Design Process—lots and lots of free-hand possibilities
  Once you've sketched out many alternatives, then work on the computer.

I'm always surprised when designers don't take time to **design** the résumé, when they wouldn't consider avoiding preliminary sketches and thumbnails for any other piece of professional work.

You aren't a graphic designer? That's OK. You still have skill in design, a feel for the look of a piece, and for the design considerations on this page.

Remember: 3 categories *(with options for others)*
1. Skills
2. Education
3. Experience
   Optional: ~honors or associations
   ~objectives (make sure they aren't limiting)

Here are some samples:

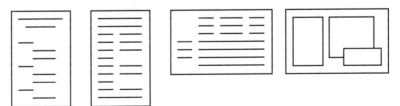

You're not a graphic designer, but you want your letterhead to be distinctive? The possibilities are endless. Have fun!

Some things to remember: All your marketing documents need to have the *same look* including

- the same letterhead
- in the same place on each document
- the same logo, if you have one
- the same fonts
- the same color
- the same margins
- the same format

A readable *font size* is 12 point for your letterhead, 10 point for the body copy. No smaller than 8 point. Fonts vary in size. Use **Times New Roman** equivalent for serif fonts and **Arial** equivalent for sans serif fonts to determine appropriate size.

Here are some letterhead options done in a widely distributed word processing program:

- *Flush your letterhead left*

Barney Jones
1625 Anystreet, Anytown, Anystate 09365
p. 222.222.2222 f. 222.222.2233 e. barneydesigns@any.com

- *or use a flush right justification*

Barbara Jones
1625 Anystreet, Anytown, Anystate 09365
p. 222.222.2222 f. 222.222.2233 e. bardesigns@any.com

- *or use a centered justification*

Billy Babcock
1625 Anystreet, Anytown, Anystate 09365
p. 222.222.2222 f. 222.222.2233 e. babcockdesigns@any.com

- *Spread out the letters of your name with a space in between each letter.*
- *Change the color on the capital letters if you want to.* (Notice how those different value letters appear smaller? You might have to change them to a larger point.)

J U N E   J O H N S O N
1625 ANYSTREET, ANYTOWN, ANYSTATE 09365
P. 222.222.2222 F. 222.222.2233 E. JUNEDESIGNS@ANY.COM

- *Vary the weight (roman, bold, italic, italic bold) in each of the lines or within your name.*

Preston Smyth
1625 Anystreet, Anytown, Anystate 09365
p. 222.222.2222 f. 222.222.2233 e. pressedesigns@any.com

Beth Jasparetti
1625 Anystreet, Anytown, Anystate 09365
p. 222.222.2222 f. 222.222.2233 e. bethdesigns@any.com

- **Use outsized capital letters** by changing the font size for one letter.

B. J. Garcia
1625 Anystreet, Anytown, Anystate 09365
p. 222.222.2222 f. 222.222.2233 e. bjgdesigns@any.com

Arthur Sung

1625 Anystreet, Anytown, Anystate 09365

p. 222.222.2222 f. 222.222.2233 e. sungdesign@any.com

- **Use a line to capture interest**, and change its color, weight or character.

Moira Tuttle
1625 Anystreet, Anytown, Anystate 09365
p. 222.222.2222 f. 222.222.2233 e. mtdesigns@any.com

Robert Nathan
1625 Anystreet, Anytown, Anystate 09365
p. 222.222.2222 f. 222.222.2233 e. robdesigns@any.com

Janice Opperman

1625 Anystreet, Anytown, Anystate 09365
p. 222.222.2222 f. 222.222.2233 e. janicedesigns@any.com

- ***Separate the name from the address with color.***

B'yrun McCullough
1625 Anystreet, Anytown, Anystate 09365
p. 222.222.2222 f. 222.222.2233 e. B'ydesign@any.com

Sabina Black
1625 Anystreet, Anytown, Anystate 09365
p. 222.222.2222 f. 222.222.2233 e. binadesigns@any.com

- ***Create a box around the name and address*** and backfill the box with color, graduations, and/or texture.

T r a c y   T r e m a y n e
1625 Anystreet, Anytown, Anystate 09365,
p. 222.222.2222 f. 222.222.2233 e. tracedesigns@any.com

Benton Baker
1625 Anystreet, Anytown, Anystate 09365
p. 222.222.2222 f. 222.222.2233 e. bendesigns@any.com

- **_Stack the letterhead in a two column setup (small column for letterhead, large column for body copy)._**

● **Juliette Beauville**
1625 Anystreet, Anytown, ST 09365
p. 222.222.2222, f.   222.222.2233
e. julesdesigns@any.com

If your letterhead is formatted to take up one thin column with the body text to take up the other wider column, _then your business card_ will probably be in the vertical format to adopt the same _look_.

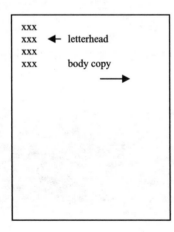

- ***Use the "draw" capacity in the word processing software to draw a circle or a square, and color it at the beginning of your letterhead.***

● **Simon Steinberg**
  1625 Anystreet, Anytown, Anystate 09365
  p. 222.222.2222   f. 222.222.2233   e. simondesigns@any.com

■ Bernadette Wayasaki
1625 ANYSTREET, ANYTOWN, ANYSTATE 09365
P. 222.222.2222 f. 222.222.2233 f. BWDESIGNS@ANY.COM

For more advanced techniques

- Use scanning software and hardware to layer images or characters from your portfolio up one side like a film strip (top or bottom are OK, too)

- Use your own logos and marks as icons to lead the eye down the page. (*Refrain* from using clip art if you are in an art or design program — you design the marks!)

- Use one of your own images as a watermark, taking care that it does not overwhelm the written communication (use no more than a 10-12% saturation or intensity for a watermark so that is does not interfere with the readability of the body copy of your résumé).

Readability and clarity are a must for your letterhead.

Have a great time creating your own "says something about you" letterhead!

A Vita for an art professional is like a *curriculum vitae* for an academic. It can also be labeled *Credits*. **It is used in all *creative industries***: TV/Film, Gaming (Computer Animation), Fine Craft, Illustration, Graphics, Advertising, Architecture, Interior Design, Theatre, Fine Arts, among many others. A Vita lists *trade-related* jobs, clients or shows you've been invited to or participated in, or been juried into. It lists:

- CD-ROM you've authored or created;

- multi-media projects you've worked on;

- plays you've participated in; or

- stores or houses you've designed.

You see? This is your professional work history.

- List in your credits *reverse chronological* order. The most recent first, completed by least recent.

- Been in industry so long that this runs for pages? Keep a collective list, but you may offer a **Selected List** or **Selected Recent List** to hit the highlights.

- It may include your education and current professional associations, but its *primary focus is to list professional accomplishments.*

Uses? Sales tools for galleries, stores, art directors, artists representatives, clients, department or institution, press kit. Additions to the Vita might be a short one-page biography. One follows this section as an example.

Make a list your clients and what you did for them. Don't forget to use *active verbs*.

The work of the individual still remains the part that moves mankind forward. —Igor Sikorsky

Sample Vita or Credits

L'Tasha R. McManus
6567 Front Street, Berkshire Island, WA 98125
p. 425.678.9234, e. LRM@tashdesigns.com, www.tashdesigns.com

Recent Work

2001

- Comprehensive Corporate Identity Package, XYT Corporation, Bellevue, WA
- Safety Brochure, Berkshire Island Fire Department
- Poster Series, United Way of King County, Support Campaign
- Website and comprehensive identity package, Special FX.com,
- Package and Boxing System, LocalChocolates.com
- Website development, comprehensive identify package, WomenSport

2000

- Advertising campaign, product launch, Local Legends
- Sales promotion campaign, production of sales training CD, Local Legends
- Packaging and point of sale campaign, Vintage Soaps & Vinegars
- Buns of Berkshire, Promotional Calendar, Berkshire Island Fire Department
- Website development, Service Exchange, a senior citizens volunteer network

Teaching

- Instructor, Website Development, Website Management, HTML,
  The Art Institute of Seattle 1997–present
- Instructor, Graphic Design, Seattle Central Community College, 1996 – 1997

Education

- MA, Whole Systems Design, Antioch University –Seattle, 1996
- BA, Graphic Design, University of Washington, 1990

Portfolio and Complete List of Credits:

- Available for Inspection at www.tashdesigns.com/portfolio

Here is a sample of a short biography offered to clients, galleries, stores, artists representatives as a sales tool, and **as part of a press kit**. Mine was developed at the request of the galleries who wanted more than the dry facts of a Vita. It can also be the basis for your One Minute Newsbrief as a response to the typical interview question: *Tell me about yourself* (known as the *TMAY* question) in the section that follows. *The benefit in developing one yourself is that you* control *what you say* and *how you say it.*

Here's a sample:

I grew up in Claremont, California in the '50s and '60's in orange grove country, where my mother was Director of Public Events for the Claremont Colleges and my father was an electrical engineer for Kaiser Steel. Many artists were working at Scripps College or in the Pomona Valley at the time and were not only household names there, but family friends. Their work and their work ethic were just part of the air there — worthy of acquisition and discussion. All these artists and craftsmen worked through their own design ideas, listened to their own muse, and many taught their philosophy of life through art. I teach now, too, and try to follow their example in passing on the philosophy of a life in art. It's a way of imparting a legacy.

I am aware as I write this that all these people I emulate are men, and I am a woman. And a woman often must balance her art with her family and the financial demands of living. My grandmother, a potter, did not pursue her art, to her detriment, and I'm aware that I carry her frustration at the limitations of her times on my shoulders. I've worked in production fiber, making bags and accessories from ethnic textiles, employed 8 sub-contractors, and worked 60 hour weeks. The limitations of production in "neo-ethnic" textiles pushed me to move into work in clay. The success of the medallions I attached to my pots prompted a move to metal, and while I still work there, I've also expanded into colored pencil drawings. I'll probably change media again. I see the expressive content as constant, although the means of expression changes. I thrive on learning new techniques and exploring new possibilities. I love teaching and the dynamics involved in the classroom. I learn more from my students than they do from me, I'm sure. I was so fortunate as a child to have several encounters with exemplary teaching, and I strive to honor my mentors. Teaching informs my art and life, and vice versa.

My constant life struggle is to balance my studio work with teaching, family, writing, and the rest of my interests. I live on an island in the Puget Sound in a grove of alders, within sight of a lovely, active harbor. I'm married to my childhood sweetheart (even though we both lived a couple of lifetimes and existences in the 15 years between our engagement and marriage), and have 2 daughters who are talented, compassionate, intelligent, and people I'm delighted to know.

My working methods are as follows: I carry a design book with me always. New work occurs to me, and I draw variations for several months, working out details and production problems. When I finally start producing, most of the problems have been eliminated, and the designs are solid. I rarely do work I haven't explored through design process first, as I find it wastes time on ideas not fully evolved. I haven't pinpointed when my mind is most open to design, but certain things I know are triggers: live contemporary dance performances; nature and history programs on PBS; museum visits; light on land and sea. There are times when I can't draw fast enough, and times when all I can do is sweep the studio. I've learned to let each of these times have its own place.

My hope is to honor the gifts I've give been given and to share those I've acquired —and to keep on keepin' on.

Persuasive Cover Letter
A persuasive cover letter is the same idea as a sales letter, because, after all, you're trying to "sell" the skills offered by **you**, the corporation.

These letters contain three main parts:

1. *Introduction:* who are you and why are you writing? Reflect the job advertisement, if that prompted you to write to this company.

    Sample:

    - **Scenario A**. *Your corporate lean toward green design attracted my attention during recent research for a class I'm taking at Anycity School of the Arts on the industry.*

    - **Scenario B**. *Animation grabbed my attention as a child and has yet to let go. The leadership role your company has taken in the industry prompts me to inquire about internships available for the fall.*

2. *Rationale/pitch*: Demonstrate how what you have to sell will benefit the company you're writing to. You will restate *in sentence form* those qualifications which you list in your résumé. The cover letter, therefore, should *directly reflect your résumé*. On your résumé, your skills are reflected in single words or short phrases, but in the cover letter you use complete sentences and paragraphs to describe those same skills.

    - **Scenario A:** *Several projects in school have been related to environmentally sound practices in the building industry as well as the disposal of environmentally hazardous materials. I'd like to apply my research and education to real world situations.*

    Expand from here. Include classes you've taken which relate to the jobs this client takes, or how your internship experience is relevant to this client.

If you think you can, you can. If you think you can't, you're right.
—Mary Kay Ash

- **Scenario B**: *I've focused my education on animation, and as my résumé suggests, have completed several projects in Softimage and 3D Studio Max. My work has application both in advertising as well as gaming.*

Expand from here. Include classes and projects you've completed which relate.

3. **Call to action**: You, the sender, will call to discuss the letter. Make sure *if you say you are going to call* at a specific time, you *do so*! A specific time should be set so the person does not have to hang around all day waiting for a call. It used to be enough to say, "If you are interested in my résumé, please call at your convenience." But now, as the marketplace gets more competitive, you cannot take a passive approach to your own career. Further, if you take a passive approach on your own behalf, where you at least have self-interest pressing you to act, what will you do for an employer?

- **Scenarios A & B**: *Thank you for taking the time to review my résumé. I will call your office on Tuesday, August 19 at 10 A.M. to discuss any suggestions (or opportunities) you may have.*

If your product or services are not needed at this particular company, **ask the next questions:**

- Are there any other questions I should be asking?
- Is there anyone else I should be talking to?
- What would you do in my shoes?

Other Considerations

In the United States, cover letters always accompany (cover) résumés sent to companies when searching for a job. *Make sure the letterhead matches your résumé, and that your skills are represented on both sheets*, in case one goes to a department head and one goes to the personnel department.

This letter *should be addressed to a specific person* **of interest**, not "Sir/ Madam": If you care enough to work for this company, you care enough to call to find out to whom the letter should be addressed.

If you are in a visual discipline (any kind of art or design), *make sure your résumé and cover letter reflect your attention to **detail and design***.

Don't forget that you are interviewing the company as much as you are being interviewed, so come prepared to ask questions about: the company's operations, the board of directors' stated views and policies, and benefits this company brings to the marketplace. **Research the company** (you know how to do this now). Read its annual reports (ask the librarian at your local library or go online), inform yourself.

Be prepared and be *enthusiastic*.

The essence of your marketing effort.

Any Student
1234 A Street, Anytown, PA 45627
p. 222.333.4444, e. anydesigns@designet.org

May 31, 20__

Ms. Benita Martinez
MB Designs
1654 S Street, Anytown, PA 45627

Re: Summer internship

Dear Ms. Martinez:

Your presentation on green design at the recent ASID meeting was inspiring.
As an interior design student nearing graduation, I'd like to learn more about
an environmentally sound approach to professional practice.

I have several qualifications that might interest you. I am bilingual (Mandarin
and English), having grown up with both English and Mandarin speakers.
I am detail oriented and work well with a team. I have a 3.8 GPA in my design
classes, and have a part-time job at DesignFibres in the Design Center.

Thank you for reviewing my résumé and Sample Sheet. I will call you at
9:00 A.M. on Thursday, June 16 to discuss any suggestions you may have.

Cordially,

Any Student

enclosure: Sample Sheet
cc: file

☑ **Letterhead**: Your name, address, and phone. Should match your résumé letterhead.

☑ **Date**: Write it out to avoid confusion: May 31, 20__.

☑ **Address block:** Name (Mr./Ms.), title, company, address.

☑ **Re: regarding what subject?** Animation intern? Ink and Painter? *This is a routing designator as the mail may be opened by a receptionist or mailroom clerk.*

☑ **Dear** Ms._____: Unless this person is a friend, always address him/her by the last name. Ends with a colon.

☑ **Paragraph #1** *Introduction:* Who *are* you and why are you writing?

☑ **Paragraph #2** *Rationale/Pitch:*
  - Qualifications and skills from your résumé *in sentence form*.
  - Put your experience in: classes; or industry related work; or freelance jobs; or even your experience with customer service and teamwork at a fast-food restaurant.

☑ **Paragraph #3** *Call to action:*
  - You will follow this résumé and cover letter up with a call to discuss your résumé and/or ask for a referral.

☑ **Closing:** Cordially, Sincerely, Never...Love!

☑ **Enclosure**: If there is one (résumé, recommendations, samples, color copies of your work, SASE, etc.).

☑ **cc:** carbon copy (outdated terminology, but still used for hard copies). Use it for the names of others to whom you are routing the letter.

Thank you letters are called *Follow-up Letters,* meaning they conclude a business transaction or meeting.

Thank you letters have *two functions*:

1.   It is the polite, courteous thing to do.
2. Thank you notes and letters are yet another legitimate chance to get your name in front of a potential client or employer.

Thank you letters are like tying the knot at the top of a balloon to hold in the air. With the knot tied, the balloon is complete, a fully expressed idea. And the same holds true if you *don't* tie the knot—*or send the thank you letter or follow-up letter*—eventually the air will flow out of the balloon.

The balloon had potential, but untied, its potential will not be reached. **Thank you letters tie the knot, completing a business transaction and opening the door for future satisfactory transactions.** *Why would you miss the opportunity* to conclude business transaction satisfactorily and do everything you can to maintain a good business contact and a good name for you, the corporation?

Thank everyone who has taken time to talk to you, to help you *in any way*. After all, s/he has taken a chunk of her/his time to help you out. Everyone—**everyone**—appreciates being thanked for effort extended.

Thank everyone you interview with not only keep your name in front of them, but to *restate and reinforce your interest in the job* as well as *reinforcing your specific qualifications* which fit the client, job, or company.

Thank you notes should be written *any* time someone helps you in any way:
- in networking situations,
- in your informational interviews (phone call, e-mail, in person) and Lead Is
- references or letters of recommendations
- any lead you receive.

When in doubt as to whether you *should* write a thank you note or letter—**do it**. Write one.

Hints:

- Be sure to spell check, grammar check.
- Keep these people's names.
- Invite them to your graduation portfolio show.
- Can you think of a downside to this???

Hand written note or formal business letter?

There really is no specific rule about this, although handwritten notes are rare in business. Perhaps a handwritten note would be appropriate when you've served on a committee together or when you have *more* than a business relationship—working out together, having a personal lunch (not a business lunch), serving on a school committee, or fundraising together. There can be no mistakes in spelling or grammar. Use spell-check and grammar-check.

You really cannot go wrong with a business letter generated on a computer. *With a business letter,* you can:

- control the tone, spelling, and grammar;
- remind the recipient of the circumstances of the call;
- use them as follow-up and reinforcement;
- keep a copy on file;
- keep a formatted letter on disk which you can customize for each client/job.

Additionally, **thank you letters can be used for other types of follow-up:**

- after a client meeting;
- as an introduction to a sales letter;
- to notify clients/employers of results of job search, or research, etc.;
- to keep networking open;
- to reward co-workers.

They take that little extra bit of effort which results in long-term and long-lasting *positive* relationships.

Our life is what our thoughts make it. —Marcus Aurelius

Why not scan one of your images from your Sample Sheet or spray-adhesive a color copy of your designs onto one side of card stock and hand write a thank you note?

- or design a banner to be affixed to the top fold of a business letter?
- or include your latest work scanned into your letterhead?

Keep printed copies of all your business correspondence in case you need to refer to it after you change your software (and you will change software as time goes by!).

Letterhead: Your Name Goes Here
Complete Address, City, State, Zip
Phone, E-mail

Today's Date

Mr./Ms. First and Last Name (confirm spelling), Title goes here
Company Name
Address
City, State, Zip, Country (if out of the country)

Dear Mr./Ms. (who did you interview?) Last Name Only:

Thank you for taking the time to discuss _____
_____
_____

with me yesterday. I talked to my Portfolio instructor today about incorporating some of your suggestions. I appreciate both the information and the encouragement.

I can't wait to put all I've learned to work.

Cordially (Sincerely, — but not Love Ya!),

Sign your full name here

enclosure: résumé and Sample Sheet
cc: file

Scenario:

Student Salina S. Guterson is completing her final quarter in college. From her Informational Interviews, she has located a design professional who is willing to take the time to look at her portfolio. This person is now part of her network, and she wants to maintain contact with him.

With these 3 thank you letters, written over a period of 4 months, she has:

- kept her network informed of her progress;

- let him know she secured an internship;

- let him know when she'll graduate;

- followed up on suggestions;

- secured an interview with him;

- *and* thanked him for the time he's invested in her career.

These contacts are polite, non-intrusive, and yet informative and positive. **Try it!** You'll be pleasantly surprised at the results.

Salina has done an
informational interview
and has written a
thank you note.

Salina S. Guterson
8953 Rose Avenue, Bainbridge Island, WA 98110
p: 206.842/1223 f: 206.842.4123 e: salinasg@designmail.com

May 16, 20_____

Mr. Gary Eperson, Partner
Moberg-Eperson Architects
2658-B W. Commodore Way
Seattle, WA 98199

Dear Mr. Eperson:

Thank you for taking the time to discuss the current marketplace in
space planning and interior design. I not only appreciate your
perspective on the Seattle design scene, but your comments have
given me more direction in charting my own future.

I will follow up on the suggestions you made regarding my portfolio,
and have contacted the firms you pinpointed for possible internships.
I have an appointment to talk to the Human Resources Director at
JBQ later this week.

I look forward to putting my talent and enthusiasm to work
when I graduate.

Cordially,

Salina S. Guterson

enclosure: Sample Sheet
cc: file

Salina S. Guterson
8953 Rose Avenue, Bainbridge Island, WA 98110
p: 206.842/1223 f: 206.842.4123   e: salinasg@designmail.com

July 15, 20_____

Mr. Gary Eperson, Partner
Moberg-Eperson Architects
2658-B W. Commodore Way
Seattle, WA 98199

Dear Mr. Eperson:

Enclosed is a color copy of the plan you suggested I reconstruct during our discussion last May. I've sent the supporting documents as well since together they earned me an A in my portfolio class (or a commission from student studio or the praise of my department chair). Thank you once again for your advice.

I'm working on an internship at the Cortner Partnership in their resource room, which I'm enjoying thoroughly, and am anticipating my graduation in October.

Sincerely,

Salina S. Guterson

Enclosure: plan, support documents, Sample Sheet
cc: file

Sample 2: (2 months later)

Salina has gotten an internship, has taken the suggestion of her interviewer, and announces her intention to graduate.

Salina has arranged and completed an interview with a company she's been in contact with. This is a *sales letter* disguised as a thank you letter. She underscores why she would be good for the job, mentioning her training and her experience.

Salina S. Guterson
8953 Rose Avenue, Bainbridge Island, WA 98110
p: 206.842/1223 f: 206.842.4123   e: salinasg@designmail.com

September 17, 20 ___

Mr. Gary Eperson, Partner
Moberg-Eperson Architects
2658-B W. Commodore Way
Seattle, WA 98199

Dear Mr. Eperson:

Thank you for taking the time to discuss the position of drafter with me yesterday and to review my portfolio.

You mentioned that most of your work is in the residential area, with a few commercial clients from time to time. I feel that my training at Arts and Design University and my experience as an intern at the Cortner Partnership in their residential design department would make me a strong candidate for the position.

Cordially,

Salina S. Guterson

cc: file

Purpose

Letters of Recommendation are written by people who can vouch for your sterling character and with whom you have a good relationship. They are offered at an interview. They differ from a reference because the recommendation is written down in letter form. They should be current (within the last 2 years).

While in the past, Letters of Recommendation were sealed and confidential, they are now fully disclosed and the property of the employee/student.

They should be written by:

- instructors and teachers;
- former or current employers or supervisors;
- volunteer associates or program coordinators;
- and intern supervisors.

They **should not** be written by relatives or friends *unless* you have worked for them.

Try to accumulate at least three Letters of Recommendation. Allow at least two weeks to receive the Letter of Recommendation.

- The request must be a personal one—a phone call or a personal visit to a classroom.
- Leave your phone number for a response.
- The person may genuinely be too busy to act upon your request in a timely manner.
- Be sure to remind the instructor, or whomever you are asking, of your name and when you were in what class.

Letters of Recommendation should be on the letterhead of the person who is writing the letter—never yours. Letters of Recommendation must be signed by the person writing the letter.

Letters of Recommendation

There are a million things in music I know nothing about. I just want to narrow down that figure. —Andre Previn

If you are an international student and want to obtain a letter of recommendation from a former employer, ask to have it faxed to you. You can then provide the translation.

Do not give away the originals. Have good copies made.

Who are you going to ask for letters of recommendation?

1.

2.

3.

A sample letter of recommendation follows for use as a footprint for those who are unsure of the content of such a letter.

Maria D. Cardenas, Ph.D

Professor, Art Department, Emerald City University

2244 University Way, Seattle, WA 98456

p. 206.789.2233, e. cardenas@ecu.edu/art

Today's Date

To Whom It May Concern:

Jason Jablonski was a student in two of my classes at Emerald City University in the Art Department: Art History and Period Studies. Jason's work was always done in a timely manner, and showed exceptional analytical and verbal skills. He also chose to complete one of the hands-on projects which was not only well researched, but well constructed with a great deal of attention to detail. Jason was a class leader in discussions, and helped other students with their work as well.

It is my pleasure to give Jason Jablonski my highest recommendation. He'd be an asset to any school or organization. If you'd like to discuss Jason's capabilities further, please do not hesitate to contact me at the numbers above.

Cordially,

Maria D. Cardenas, Ph.D

A reminder memo gently and politely jogs the memory of those who've said they'll write those letters of recommendation, but have forgotten to do so.

To:

From: Your Name goes here

Contact Number: Your phone or e-mail goes here

Thank you for agreeing to write a Letter of Recommendation for me. According to my Syllabus Addendum, it is due in class on Week 8. Please put the letter in _____ mailbox.
                                        (Instructor's Name)
Sincerely,

Sign your name here

Note the date you've sent the reminder memo and to whom:

- To: Date:

- To: Date:

- To: Date:

- To: Date:

Have you sent a *thank you note* in response? It's a must. After all, this person has taken some time out of his/her day to help you out!

Purpose

References are people who can vouch for your sterling character, and with whom you have a good relationship. When Letters of Recommendation were private and sealed, a List of References lost favor, but now that Letters of Recommedation are always positive and open, carried by the applicant, the List of References has regained favor. Quite a bit can be said by pauses and tone of voice even if the words are always positive ones.

A list is made **on your letterhead**, which includes for each reference:

- name
- complete address
- phone number
- your relationship with this person

Call or e-mail and **ask** if you can use this person as a reference, so s/he can be prepared to answer questions about you. If you are a former student, remind the instructor/professor/teacher when you attended classes and which class it was. Sometimes your references are called to check on you, and sometimes they are sent a written questionnaire.

Accumulate at least 3 references (You can duplicate your Letters of Recommendation or not, as you choose).

Whom should you ask?

- former or current employers or supervisors
- teachers, instructors, professors
- volunteer supervisors
- intern supervisor
- *not* your parents, spouse, or relatives

Do you have a job history or educational history in another name? (married/legal name change)? Indicate on your reference list if any of these people have known you under another name (such as your maiden name).

Who are you going to ask to be references?

1.
2.
3.
4.

Thank you notes sent? This is a must. This person has agreed to take some of his/her time to help you out.

- To: Date:

- To: Date:

- To: Date:

- To: Date:

A sample List of References follows.

Pete Abramowitz
6254 17th Street, Boston, MA 21654
p. 789.876.5432, e. pete_a@animators.net

List of References

1. Ms. Muriel P. Dasher, Instructor
   The School of Visual Arts
   1465 8th Avenue
   New York, New York 06254
   212.654.7895

   Ms. Dasher was my 3D Studio Max instructor.

2. Mr. Ben Weinstein, Instructor
   The School of Visual Arts
   1465 8th Avenue
   New York, New York 06254
   212.654.7895

   Mr. Weinstein was my portfolio instructor.

3. Mr. Tom Washington
   Lake Wishona Summer Camp
   Lake Wishona, WI 25607
   345.629.8546

   Mr. Washington was the camp supervisor where I taught
   canoeing and computer skills—summers 1998–2001.

Business Cards

In the United States, business people are expected to have a business card,

- which you leave with an interviewer or client,
- put into correspondence,
- give in networking situations,
- use for your clients/employer's reference,
- place in your display for portfolio review,
- and carry in your interview portfolio, etc.

These should reflect your own *corporate* identity, and should match your résumé and cover letter letterhead.

Business cards are 2" x 3.5" in format, so that each printed page has 12 cards on it in a 3 x 4 layout. Business cards in countries which have a *metric system* are *5.5 cm x 9.0 cm.*

Do not exceed this format. You want people to keep your card for reference—a little bit of your corporation at easy access on their desk or in a Rolodex. And therein lies the problem: *your card must fit in a business card file or on a Rolodex. If it is a non-standard* card, it will be separately filed and eventually tossed out.

Many accessible printing establishments print each sheet of cards for 15–20¢ depending on paper, how much of the layout work you've already done (camera-ready, it's called), and how much the printer has to do.

*Typically t*he chop (cutting the cards) is under $15 if set up according to the format:

- justified left
- 1/8" drop from the top
- 1/4" drop from the side.

Printing and cutting 250 cards should cost you less than $20 if your card is ready to print (black ink). The entire sheet should be pasted up so that the sheets can be printed and then cut. ***Check with your local printer to determine their typical set-up and prices.*** Each printer will be different.

Do not use the *tear-away* cards developed for computer printers. The perforations always show and the results are very naive. Aaaagggghhhh!

Sure, print your cards on card stock on the computer printer.

- Use a **sharp** blade and a metal straight edge, and cut them yourself.

- The *printing must look sharp* and clean, however, and not fuzzy.

- The cuts must be on the grid, be sharp and clean (do not even **think** about using a paper cutter).

- When you design your card, leave out the framing line so you have some latitude in your cuts. If you frame your card with a line, the cuts must be perfectly spaced.

Skills designator

 Under your name goes a skills designator, often the name of the program you're studying. Until you've actually **worked** in the profession you're claiming knowledge of, it is important **not** to put an "*er*" or "*or*" at the end of the words, as follows:

Put:	Do Not Put:
Interior Design	Interior Design**er**
Graphic Design	Graphic Design**er**
Computer Animation	Computer Animat**or**
Fashion Design	Fashion Design**er**

The marketplace frowns on exaggerating experience if you have none.
This saves you having to answer the embarrassing question:

- *Oh, where have you worked?*
- Or *what kind of work have you done?*
- Or *who have you worked with?*

Now, design the *look* of your card, keeping in mind your corporation's overall design presentation package. Some considerations are:

- portrait or landscape format?
- name in larger type or different font?
- use of negative space on the card?

Try to stay within your capabilities on the computer or in paste-up
or trade some skill with a graphic designer. Look in the library under *Art Directors annuals* or *Graphis annuals* for terrific ideas.

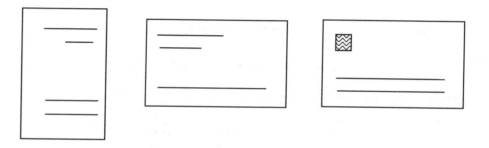

Yours? Sketch out your ideas:

It is becoming more common to submit a *color collage* of samples of your work with your résumé and cover letter—sort of a mini portfolio on one page—called a **Sample Sheet.**

The purpose of constructing a color Sample Sheet is:

- to present your work *within the critical first five minutes* of the interview, when decisions (not) to hire are typically made

- to have a **leave behind**—to leave a relatively inexpensive copy of your work with the client for future reference (freelance or contract work?)

- to accompany your résumé and cover letter for out-of-state work.

Too many people overvalue what they are not and undervalue what they are. —Malcolm Forbes

This Sample Sheet *must be* **designed**, just as your graphic presentation is designed.

- How will you organize the material for impact/emphasis?

- How will you determine the positive and negative space?

- How will you work with symmetry and asymmetry in balance?

- How about the harmonies to lead the eye in circulation?

Your Sample Sheet needs to have **the same *look*** as the rest of your graphic presentation.

Examples:

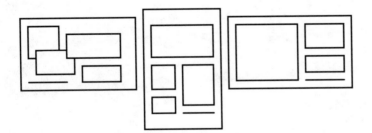

It's your turn: do at least 5 thumbnails to layout your collage on the side of this page.

Techniques of construction vary: You can

- Scan images with a business card imported.

- Place photographic prints of your work arranged around your business card and color copy it all together.

- Import slides and arrange them around your business card (many reproduction houses will do this).

- Call the photographer or scan in your documents onto a disk.

- Call your local reprographic house to see which procedure will work best for you:

  - Slides to color copy

  - Slides to scanner and then burned onto a CD

  - Prints on the bed of the color copier with your business card, color copied

  - Scanned images with your letterhead on disk

- Of course, if you have access to this equipment, construct your own and print it out. Make sure to get **crisp edges on the images** and a high dpi or ppi.

Your Sample Sheet should be constantly updated with your most recent work, and sent to prospective clients and/or employers on a regular basis, referring to your entire portfolio on your Website.

Your portfolio presents what you know how to do; the sum of your life's experiences are represented in it. Once you have assembled it, secure it!

Your Portfolio

Your portfolio presents *what you know how to do*. It should include several types of documents:

- competency in a variety of computer programs demonstrated
- several styles shown
- several media explored
- several types of hypothetical clients satisfied
- several applications of design demonstrated

Experience is not what happens to a person; it's what a person does with what happens to him or her.
—From Aldous Huxley

Size

There is a trend *away* from huge presentation boards to ones which will fit into an 11"x17" portfolio for several reasons:

- they can be scanned into a computer and sent to a client by modem;
- they can be carried on an airplane without buying an extra seat;
- they can be sent via Federal Express in a standard sized box;
- and they can be handled with ease.

CD-ROM

Many creatives put their portfolios on CD-ROM, which may become an industry standard. Unless you have a laptop with you for presentation (Why not rent one, charge up the batteries, put your programs on it, and have it ready for presentation —can you say "rolling black-outs"?), it is important to have hard copies of the images with you as well. Indeed, **always take hard copies** of your artwork with you (printed on a color printer or copier). Put your business card on the back of each.

It should reflect the same design concept as all other graphic presentations to leave with the client and/or interviewer. Why? You want your visual work to accompany your résumé to set you apart from your competition, and you want your work to be kept on file for possible contract or freelance opportunities.

Do not arrive at a client presentation or at a job interview with your portfolio CD and no hardware.

- You cannot assume that the company will have the same software you do and can open the files;
- that the company will have an extra computer for viewing your CD, or
- that the electricity will be available for your presentation (again, those pesky rolling black-outs).

Bring your own laptop for the presentation.

- You don't own one? Rent one!
- Load your programs and portfolio.
- Take extra batteries. Power them up.
- Take the whole kit with you.
- If you are taking an airplane to make the presentation, do **not** check the laptop or your portfolio as luggage.

Websites

Many creatives establish a Website to show their work. Make sure that if your target audience is world-wide in nature, that you are *culturally sensitive.*

The **up-side** of a Website is

- of course, that you have a great deal of exposure to those who might not have access to your work otherwise;
- you can form an informal network with those whose work is similar or whose interests are similar through *links;*
- and you have access to e-tail (rather than traditional retail) opportunities.

The **downside** of a Website is

- it must be maintained;
- it must be protected from hacking;
- you have little copyright protection;

- your links must remain compatible with your material and inoffensive to a world-wide audience;
- you cannot assume that when you mention your Website in your corporate documents that buyers, clients, directors, producers, etc. *will actually take the time to visit it*.
- security: everyone with access to the Web has access to your contact numbers (and, if you post it, your address and phone number).

To give yourself the best opportunity, do not overlook a *Sample Sheet* that can be handled, filed, and distributed in traditional ways for those clients and customers who are still traditionalists—yes, they are legions of them still out there.

There is *no downside to having both* a Sample Sheet for distribution as well as a Website for a tandem *traditional media* and *new media* approach.

The order of your portfolio

Put the items which reflect the work the company does *first* to demonstrate that you can work in that style. How do you find out about that style? Research, research, research:

- periodicals,
- Art Director annuals,
- professional association inquiries, calling to ask where the client is published.

Showing Your Best Work: There are several schools of thought.

1. **Show the best first**. Open with **wow**! Show work that has won you prizes or honors.

2. **Save your best pieces for last** to create **the big impression**. Finish
   with a *bang!* Just to ensure that your best piece is seen, why not have that
   Sample Sheet include your best piece that you're saving for last, so if the
   interview is concluded early due to business demands, the interviewer has
   already seen your best? The Sample Sheet underlines your prowess in
   technique, program and image, and allows you to leave a great impression
   behind to work for your corporation when you're not there.

   - *The phone rings: the interviewer answers, looks at his/her watch and
     concludes the interview by apologizing for a shortened interview, and
     asking to see the pieces on the Sample Sheet.*

   - You don't have to fumble. You know it's at the end of your presentation.
     You can calmly take it out for a closer view, knowing that the rest of your
     work is demonstrated on the Sample Sheet that you are leaving behind.

3. **Show work that is compatible with the client's work first.** Your immediate
   task is to keep yourself in the running, so you will want to have work that
   demonstrates that you can do work the client will want you to do, based on the
   work they already do. No matter what you *say* about what you can do, you
   must have visual proof that you can do the work required of you by this client
   or company.

Other considerations

Take only your *first–rate* work. It's better to have a few first rate pieces than
several you have to apologize for. Of course, you'll update often.

Portfolio presentations are not the place for dissembling.

- *I could have done better if I... I really wanted to do that but my teacher
  insisted on this...This was clean until my dog sat on it.* **No whining.**

- *Never* tell the client what is wrong with the piece. *Demonstrate what is
  good about it* and how you exceeded expectations when you constructed
  it. Tell where, in terms of design, this piece really works.

What is your best work?

- Your best work is the one you feel the most enthusiastic about at the moment. If you showed your portfolio to 5 designers, would you get the same feedback from each? Probably not.

- Give up that immature approach that says "I don't like any of my work." Why are you in this profession? An honest, mature approach demands that each piece you work on is the best you can do.

Continually upgrade your portfolio. It will always represent the best you can do at the time. *But...*

- Resist perpetually fussing with your portfolio so that is never quite ready, and you have a sad excuse for not pursuing your dreams.

- Learn new computer programs as soon as you can and keep demonstration pieces of each program you know in your portfolio.

Practice showing your portfolio, taking out each piece and discussing its positive aspects.

- Sounds silly, doesn't it?

- Just as you'd prepare any presentation, prepare this one. Practice.

Keep your portfolio wrapped in plastic *so food or smoke odors do not permeate the room when you open it (a garbage bag should do).*

- Imagine a *wow!* visual impact and a *yuck!* odor.

- Resist the temptation, however, to put one of those odor sweetners in your bag.

Keep a record

- Take slides or scan your pieces.

- Keep a disk of your artwork.

- Date them (and your sketches in your sketchbook in case of do-not-compete clauses with your employer) and note to whom you sold the image so that you can retrieve them later.

Edit your portfolio *for each interview or client* presentation, so that work that interests the company is demonstrated within the 5 minutes of the portfolio presentation portion of an interview (see the Interview segment on page 178 for timing considerations.) *For instance:*

- If you are interviewing for a toy design position, place the toy design work you've done first and the environmental design work at the back of the portfolio.

- If you are showing your children's cartooning work to a company with similar interests, the heavy metal album cover you did will be at the end of your portfolio. You may even decide to leave it out of this presentation.

Take your sketchbook along.

Many design students create a concept book with selected images taken from ideation to demonstrate their process skills. Concepts placed in a job-book look great, but a whole book of disconnected concepts seems sterile.

Personally, I prefer to see the complete sketchbook rather than a sanitized concept book. Here's why:

- With a sketchbook, I can see how dominant a personality the portfolio instructor has. I can see if the work in the sketchbook is consistent with the work shown in the portfolio.

- What I like to see is the tattered sketchbook, the one with dog-eared corners because it has been carried everywhere, the spaghetti and coffee stains, cat pawprints, and grocery lists.

- I want to see how a designer thinks, how s/he visualizes concepts, and how s/he fits that into a life well lived.

- I get a glimpse into the personality as well as the skills of the designer and some sense of how this person will fit into the scene at the office.

Relax!

You've prepared a terrific portfolio. Think about how fun it is to show fascinating people your wonderful work.

What order will yours be in?

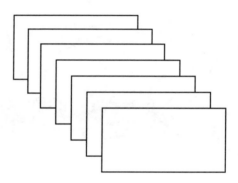

Protect your portfolio from life's little mishaps.

IV: The Interview

The purpose of the interview

Whether you're looking for a job with a company *or you're planning to freelance*, you'll have to meet with a prospective employer or client *and show who you are and what you can do*.

There is little difference in the two situations, except how the money is going to be distributed: in paychecks over time as an employee, or in big chunks at one time as a freelancer; and who is going to pay the employer's part of the social security tax: the company in case of an employee, or you, in the case of freelance.

Approach

Your interview is a **planned and organized presentation** *to sell yourself and your skills to an employer or client.*

- Your résumé, business card, list of references, and Sample Sheet represent your *sales* **documents**.

- Your **interview** is your *sales* **presentation**. It is part of the marketing process.

Approach all interviews *prepared*, so *you* can turn the interview into a conversation where information can be exchanged.

- Visit the Website for the firm or client.

- Go to your trade journal Website to see if any articles have been written about the company or its business principles or clients.

- Use the library to find recent trade magazines to read articles in the broad subject area.

As I have gotten braver, I have censored myself less.
—Gretchen Cryer

Use the library's resources to find current information about the company. Local and national business trade magazines and/or newspapers often have year-end books of lists about the top companies in your area. Example: *Puget Sound Business Journal's Book of Lists.*

Create an **"interview kit."** Keep it stocked with:

- Names, addresses, phone numbers of former employers, and references to aid you in filling out an employment application.
- Extras of **all** your graphic presentation (résumé, Sample Sheet, business cards, List of References)
- Letters of Recommendation
- Identification, Social Security number, and proof of work permit if required
- Breath mints and extra panty hose
- Maps of the area
- Two pens (one blue, one black)

Qualities employers look for

The most *important trait employers look for* during an interview is: ***enthusiasm,*** followed by
- good grammar,
- eye contact,
- body posture,
- confidence,
- flexibility,
- timeliness,
- and willingness to work on a team.

Preparation

Know and be yourself. This is why we spent time on goals, on personality tests and on values sorters, so that you would be armed with information that will guide you to find companies and a client base that suits who you are.

You know your likes and dislikes, your strengths, weaknesses and career path to your goals. *Accent the positive.*

*Find out as much as possible about the organization and position. Anticipate questions and **prepare your responses*** so that even if your mind goes blank, intelligent answers come out of your mouth.

Know your portfolio.

- Be able to discuss *each piece* in terms of the assignment given, how you *exceeded* requirements, strengths of design or concept, craftsmanship, print quality, etc.

- Find out what kind of work this group does and *do some work that is similar to it*, so you can prove that you can fit into their approach.

- *Prepare your portfolio so that work which is compatible with this firm's work is **first*** *in order.* If you are determined to save your "best" piece for last (they should all be your best!), you should have a **Sample Sheet** including that piece to present with your résumé so *if the interview is shortened* for any reason, this piece will still get a show.

- ***Take only your first-rate work***. Interviews are a whine-free zone. Take nothing you have to apologize for or make excuses for.

- You *may* want to consider taking a 2nd quarter project to show how much you've improved and demonstrate your quick learning capabilities. *(Get me now while I'm cheap!)* This is a judgment call.

- **Take extra copies** of
  - your résumé
  - your letters of recommendation
  - your references
  - your business cards.
  - and a **color Sample Sheet** of your work.

- Be ready with the offer to leave information with them.

- Why take extra copies? Perhaps the person you were scheduled to interview with is sick; your résumé is locked in his/her desk. The new interviewer can't get a copy to discuss with you. *Take extra copies!*

- Should you have a business card, even though you have your résumé? Sure! They go in the card file for reference and   contract work.

Employment application

You will be asked to fill out an employment application even if you have a résumé. Why? It is a legal contract of intent and commitment.

- Read it **thoroughly** before you fill anything in and sign it. Ignorance is not a defense.

- It will probably contain a section on drug and medical testing, what happens to your samples, and how they will be evaluated.

- Attention to detail, clarity of expression, completion are issues of concern to employers.

- Have your *social security number* handy.

- Indicate if any former employers or references know you under a different name (married, remarried, legal name change).

- Check out an employment application at a local stationery store. They're legal documents, approved by your state.

Manners are like zero in arithmetic. They may not be much in themselves, but they are capable of adding a great deal of value to everything else. —Freya Stark

Other Considerations

Smile, as you are glad to have this opportunity to meet another interesting person.

Know where you are going *and how long it will take you to get there.*

- Arrive early—at least 5 minutes.
- Walk around the block if you are too early.
- *Do not be late.* There is **no** good recovery from being late. This is one of those unwritten laws in business in the United States.

Confirm appointment the day before with a phone call. Ask if you will be asked to fill out an application before the interview. Confirm the length of time to complete the application and arrive in enough time to do so.

Smoking and drinking (did I say anything about drugs or alcohol?)

- *Never smoke or drink (anything)* **in or** *right before* *the interview,* even if the opportunity is offered. This is both for the protection of your work (oops, a latte just spilled into my portfolio!) as well as to maintain a professional appearance.

- *Never,* ***never*** have alcohol on your breath.

- Avoid onions, garlic, and alcohol the night before as well. As you perspire (and you will!), the odors appear in your perspiration.

- Be aware that many companies are *required by their insurance* policies to drug test. Tests are becoming cheaper and more sophisticated. *Street wisdom* about how to cleanse and detox should be viewed with extreme skepticism. The test may require a hair sample, a blood sample, or a urine sample.

- o Hair grows 1" per month.
- o Shaving down is *not* a good idea. (What are you trying to hide?)

- Issues about the use of blood tests and other DNA tests on your samples are even now being tested in courts and will continue to be an issue during your working lifetime. Once you have given a sample, to whom does it belong? What kind of testing can be done with it?

- Can you be excluded from employment because of a DNA test that reveals that you have a predilection for early Alzheimer's disease, or a weakness for carpal tunnel, for instance?

Go to the interview alone. Leave your scruffy roommate at home, even if the roommate owns the car you arrived in.

Transportation

Some interviewers walk applicants back to their cars. The make and model will not matter, but the cleanliness will. *Everything* about you reflects your corporate attitude.

Interviewing team

Be aware that *the receptionist and other staff* may be as important to the interview team as the art director you planned to meet. Be sure to introduce yourself. Always be polite. (Remember, these people are potential clients for your *corporation*.) The interviewer may ask the other staff for their impression of you after you have left, *including the people who walk through the reception area while you're waiting.*

Multiple interviews

Be aware that *the interview process may have several parts* and that this interview is just the *first* of several. This process may take 6 weeks or so.

It is perfectly legitimate to ask how long the interview process will take. It is **not** a good idea to call and ask "How 'm I doin'?"

Presentation

Make a positive impression and sell the capabilities of *your corporation.* Many interviewers make a judgment (especially **not to hire**) **within the first five minutes.** *This is why a Sample Sheet is essential*—get it in front of the interviewer with your résumé in those crucial first 5 minutes. Try to project qualities like:

- enthusiasm
- interest
- sincerity
- willingness to work
- a team player

- initiative
- flexibility
- honesty
- dependability
- confidence

Appearance

First impressions are created by appearance. The way you dress, comb or style your hair and your posture all combine to create your *look.* Treat this like a design problem.

Be aware that failure to pay attention to these details may eliminate you before you even open your mouth or show your portfolio.

Select interview apparel that is tasteful, conservative, comfortable, and appropriate for the organization and position. Make sure it will still look good if you gain or lose 5 lbs. *Clean* this outfit and hang it in a plastic bag, knotted top and bottom, so no odors of any kind can permeate the clothing and suggest that you engage in bad habits. (Just think how your clothes smell the day after a party…).

*Dress appropriately for an interview with **this** organization.* How do you find this out? Call the receptionist and ask! This may be *different* than the daily dress of current employees of this firm. Interview clothes mimic those worn to a client meeting.

- ***This can* mean** (depending on the interviewer and circumstances):

  o   no slacks for women,

  o   no earrings for men (ask)

  o   no baseball caps or hats

  o   no exposed midriffs, even if you just got the cutest belly button pierce

  o   no T-shirts with tacky slogans (*Party till you Puke* for instance, or bands with suggestive names)—do not wear such a T-shirt under a dress shirt and assume you are safe. You're not!

  o   no jeans with holes in them

  o   no athletic shoes

Minimize jewelry including removing nose, eyebrow, and lip rings, lip and tongue studs.

Minimize cosmetics.

Cover tattoos. Whatever it takes — grow your hair, wear a collared shirt, use leg make-up, wear tights or pants, long sleeve shirts.

Conservative hemlines — skirts (if you have to tug on your hem to appear conservative, your skirt is too short for business situations) and pants

No cleavage or chest hair showing.

No nail polish or make-up for men. Conservative nail polish for women. File nails to accommodate computer work.

Do not wear cologne, aftershave, or perfume to an interview. The interviewer may be allergic or really dislike your choice of scent. Do you *really* want to be eliminated from the possible candidates because of your choice of a scent?

Be aware that the East Coast is *much* more formal than the West Coast and that *each region* has its own standards of dress. **Ask!**

Different positions at companies are required to wear different clothes. For instance:

- *an ink and painter position* could require cotton slacks, sport shirt, deck shoes or skirt, sweater and sandals for an interview;

- a *managerial position* could require sport jacket, white shirt, tie or scarf, wool slacks or skirt, and polished laced shoes.

Clean out your car. A well-known dot.com interviewer walks interviewees to his/her car to see if it is clean and well kept.

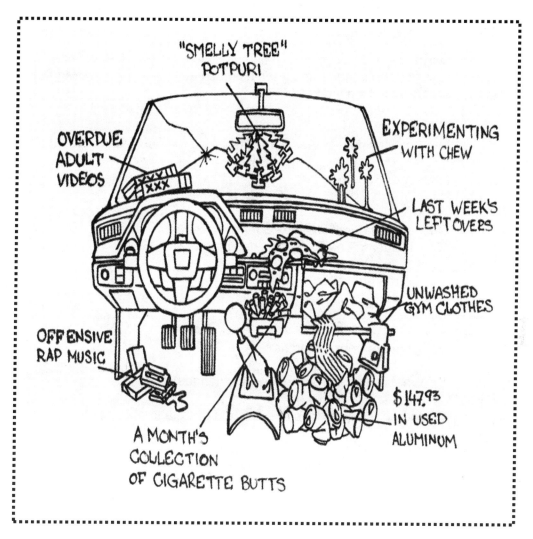

Some interviewers accompany applicants back to the car.

Timing

Interviewing is a 4-part process which *usually takes about 30 minutes.* Remember, you are interviewing them as much as they are interviewing you. Both parties are trying for a good fit.

Part 1: *5 minutes*
- Introductions, first impressions, (including the decision **not to hire**)

- Review of Résumé

Part 2: *15 minutes*
- Open ended questions (see 80+ most frequently asked questions on page 191), including The Big Four—see below.

   o Tell me about yourself.

   o Why do you want to work here?

   o What are your strengths?

   o What are your weaknesses (challenges)?

- Closed-ended questions to see if you can elaborate **past** "yes" and "no."

- Borderline inappropriate questions to see if you get rattled in stressful situations (see following sections).

- Portfolio presentation

   o **can you do this in 5 – 8 minutes?** Practice!

   o ask half way through how the interviewer is doing for time.

- Always take a full sketchbook (as an interviewer, I don't know how much the portfolio instructor has art directed your portfolio, but I can tell a great deal about you from your sketchbook: how you develop ideas, and if you can start with a kernel of an idea and develop it to completion).

- Personally (as mentioned in the section on your portfolio), I even like to see soy sauce stains, to-do lists, and cat pawprints. I like to find out about the person I'll be working with. And how dedicated you are to your work—do you carry your sketchbook everywhere? (Of course, others may feel differently.)

Part 3: *7 – 8 minutes*

- Description of position

- Description of training or orientation

- Ask for questions. (*Do you have any questions?*) Have **three** prepared (See section *Interview Questions to Ask*). If you don't have any questions, the interviewer may think you are apathetic about this opportunity. Take a notebook (tasteful) with your questions written down. You may not have time for more than one question, but you may be expected to have more.

Part 4: *2 – 3 minutes*

- Explanation of steps in the interviewing process

- Close of interview. **You say**: *Thank you for taking the time to see me. I've enjoyed meeting you.* Pick up your portfolio. Leave with grace.

*Interview timing adapted from the following resource: *How You Really Get Hired* by John L. LaFevre, p. 65-66. See Resource List included in the Addenda.

Other considerations:

Turn *off*
- your pager
- your cell phone—except in extreme cases (Your wife is in labor? What *are* you doing at an interview?)
- your alarm watch
- your electronic datebook
- anything else you have on you that plays songs, buzzes, beeps, whistles, or vibrates.

Prepare where your hands will go during your presentation, so you can relax when you are in the interview. Wash your hands and clean your nails.

Maintain eye contact, *not laser-like mind control, but genuine interest in the other person.* In fact, genuinely taking an interest in the other person is a terrific way to overcome shyness and self-consciousness.

Speak clearly and directly. Show that you are confident of your capabilities but not cocky. Express *interest* in company's work and in interviewer.

Shake hands firmly with the interviewer to begin and end the meeting with both men and women (not the bone-crusher handshake or the limp fish handshake, but a quick squeeze and release).

- Is shaking hands an inappropriate power move for an applicant? No. Shaking hands shows confidence.

- Grasping the elbow or arm with your other hand, however, **is** a power move, and is inappropriate in this circumstance.

If guidance isn't given, ask where to sit and suggest the way you would like to show your portfolio.

Bring up positive points *in response to the questions.*

Approach a closed-ended question (answerable in one or two words) as a challenge to your creativity. Have you learned to get past "yes" or "no"? Practice.

Elaborate briefly on your experience, skills, and background.

Establish your interest. *Make sure you have explained why you are interested in the position and what you have to offer.*

Know exactly what you want and what your goals are. That's why we spent time on your reverse autobiography and your values sorters. *Be realistic about them.*

Listen *to questions and answer only what is asked.*

- Do not make assumptions or ramble.

- Ask for clarification if you do not understand a question.

- Keep your answers framed by your résumé and on a professional level.

Refrain from complaining or being overly critical about previous jobs or education. Complaining reflects badly on you. Now you seem like a whiner. Remember that *your attitude* is under your complete control—probably the *only* thing you have complete control of. Construct a positive attitude, a "glass-half-full outlook." It is contagious! A positive attitude reflects well on you and draws people to you.

Before leaving the interview, find out about the next step in the process. Will additional information such as transcripts or references be needed? *Find out if there will be a second interview* and when they plan to make a hiring decision. Find out when you can expect to hear from them.

Thank *the interviewer for the time and opportunity to meet.* Write a thank you note, card, or letter to each person you interviewed with. You will be memorable.

If you are interested in the position, **say so**.

On an informational interview, **ask for referrals** and the following questions:

- What other questions should I be asking?

- What else should I be researching?

- Is there anyone you can think of I should be talking to?

Establish the fact that **you are willing to check in on a regular basis.**

Do not …

- ask about salary and benefits in the first interview.

- tell jokes (your sense of humor might be very different than that of the interviewer, but, on the other hand, establishing that you do have a sense of humor is appropriate—just not via jokes!).

- discuss your personal difficulties or life situation.

- mention any gossip or insider information you might be privy to.

- take a cell-phone call during the interview.

- chew gum or tobacco.

- smoke before or during the interview.

- leave your beeper, cell, or your timer watch on. Turn anything with tunes, bells, whistles, buzzes, beeps, and even vibrations—**off!**

Have fun!

No, really! If you approach interviewing as an *opportunity to meet professionals in your field* and as an opportunity to gather as much information as possible to aid your corporation, interviewing can be interesting, instructive, and even **fun**!

Skill and confidence are an unconquered army.
—George Herbert

*Relevant Resources – see Resource List in the Addenda:
- any books by Joyce Lain Kennedy, syndicated careers columnist for interviewing, résumé skills. Look in the *...for Dummies* series, IDG Books, Foster City, CA, 1996.
- John T. Malloy: *John T. Malloy's New Dress for Success.* New York: Warner Books, 1988.
- Janet Wallach*: Looks That Work: How to Match Your Wardrobe to Your Professional Profile and Create the Image That's Right for You.* New York: Viking, 1986.

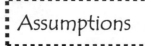

Assumption I.

Your first encounter with the employer or client is at the first interview.

- The fact is you, the corporation, have several encounters with the employer and/or client before you actually meet face-to-face, all of which speak about your attention to detail and design: your résumé and Sample Sheet, your phone call, and the message on your answering service.

So

- Take all unprofessional messages and long cuts from your favorite song *off* your answering service.

- If you are a *frequent Internet user*, arrange with a telephone company to intercept your calls with a call-back message so your potential client/employer does not meet with incessant busy signals, or, if you aren't home, with no opportunity to leave a message at all.

And

- Some companies prescreen applicants using written forms or interviews with other departments' staff members.

- Some interview groups rather than individuals during "first-round" interviews, called "cattle-calls."

- The receptionist's impression of you is usually considered and solicited. Were you cordial to the receptionist when you called to ask for information?

Assumption II.

The interviewer won't form an opinion about you *until the interview is over*.

- Most interviewers form opinions in the first 5 minutes, particularly the decision ***not to hire*. This is important to know when you are showing a portfolio.** That is why a **color Sample Sheet** is a good addition to your résumé. You can get your work in front of the interviewer immediately -- in that crucial first 5 minutes.

- Over half of the decisions to hire are based on non-verbal communication (eye contact, body language, expressions, clothing, timeliness, enthusiasm, even scent) and the interviewer's "gut" reactions.

Assumption III.

If you have the qualifications for the job, you'll be hired.

- Some things are out of your control, such as the personality of the interviewer, personal problems in the interviewer's life, unacknowledged prejudices on the interviewer's part, telephone interruptions, worklife in the office where you are interviewing, and a whole host of other things you may not be aware of.

- Jobs are rarely offered on the spot. Relax and enjoy getting to know this person. What an opportunity!

- Encourage the interviewer to call your references if you feel that the interviewer may have a hard time making a decision.

Assumption IV.

Schedule an interview anytime you can fit it in.

- Tuesday, Wednesday, or Thursday are best. Why?

- *Monday* is taken up by business which has accumulated over the weekend. It is a ***very*** *busy phone day* and your interview is likely to be interrupted several times by crises that have accumulated and need to be dealt with immediately.

- *Friday* is a "get away" day and your interviewer is probably thinking about leaving early, stocking refreshments, friends s/he's going to see, and what's happening on the weekend.

- ***Note:*** Of course, you **should** schedule on Monday or Friday *if the other days are not available*, but for **optimum** interview time, **Tuesdays, Wednesdays, and Thursdays** are the best.

Other assumptions you've encountered:

Before the interview, you need to research the company.

- Is their corporate structure one which *fits your personality, ideals, and goals*?

- Will this position fulfill your Plan A or Plan B?

- Is this position an unnecessary tangent or will it ultimately support your goals?

- Your research projects a positive image of someone who is proactive and prepared. You should *not* be asking who the company's clients and target market are. You should know this from your research. See the Resources section in the Addenda of this workbook.

Research

- What are the company's major products and services?

- How long have they been in business?

- How big is the company? Has it grown?

- Who are the company's customers?

- What is the corporate culture (what is day-to-day activity and atmosphere like)?

- What is the reputation of the company from articles in trade journals?

- Is the company privately or publicly owned? Is there a parent company that is involved in daily transactions?

- Is employee turnover high? Reasons? (Find out from a colleague at a professional organization meeting—*What do you know about XYZ Company?*)

Always do right. That will gratify some people and astonish the rest.
—*Mark Twain*

- Other items you think are important:

Resources

- Some of your research will come from your usual resources (Books of Lists, yearbooks, etc.), some will come from networking (asking people you know in the industry, at your professional association meetings, or chat room SIGS—special interest groups), and some will come from Websites.

Make note of

- Name of company
- Name of interviewer
- Address
- Phone number
- Directions to interview site
- Planned time frame for transportation

Ask the receptionist

- Will an application be filled out before the interview?

- What is the appropriate dress for the interview? (Is your interview clothing cleaned, pressed, and ready to go?)

```
..................................
:                                :
: Interview Questions to         :
:                   Ask          :
:                                :
..................................
```

Always *have at least 3 questions* prepared to ask at the end of the interview in response to:

- ***Do you have any questions?***

- WHY? You sound *interested and **enthusiastic***. Remember, that's what employers are looking for!

- If the interview is drawing to a close (usually at 30 minutes), and you haven't had a chance to ask questions, you can bring up *at least one* of your questions with this: *I have a couple of questions for you.*

Here are examples of good interview questions to ask:

- What are the day-to-day responsibilities for this position?

- What is a typical day like in the department?

- How long has this position been open?

- How long will you be interviewing?

- What is the career path for this position?

- With whom would I be working?

- To whom would I be reporting? More than one person?

- Who makes the final decision on hiring for this position?

- When do you expect that the final hiring decision will be made?

...diligence is the mother of good luck. —Benjamin Franklin

- Is there a training or orientation program for the employees? How long does it last?

- Are there any questions that you have about my background that I may clarify for you?

- May I take a tour of the facility?

- Would you like my transcripts or letters of reference transferred?

- What is the next step in the hiring process?

- Could you describe to me your typical management style and the type of employee that works well with you?

- What are some of the skills and abilities you see as necessary for someone to succeed in this job?

- What challenges might I encounter in this position?

- What areas in this job would you like improved?

- What are your major concerns that need to be addressed immediately in this job?

- Will I be working with a team or alone?

- What would a former employee say about this company?

NOTE: Questions about salary and benefits are reserved until the 2nd or 3rd interview. They are usually discussed with the Director of Human Resources.

- Good questions you've thought up:

Interview Questions to Expect

You can expect to be asked several typical questions, depending on how experienced your interviewer is.

The Big Four: There are four questions that are the most commonly asked:
1. Tell me about yourself. (TMAY)
2. Why do you want to work here?
3. What are your strengths?
4. What are your weaknesses (challenges)?

Focus on genuine and positive answers. For instance, *jail time? One of the most important and intensive learning episodes in my life.* (See Flipping a Negative to a Positive section on page 209.) Remember, **interviews are *whine-free* zones**.

Save question 1 (the TMAY question—Tell me about yourself) for the segment on page198.

Use questions 2 and 3 as a springboard for the *Strengths and Weaknesses* segment which follows on page 204.

Some of these questions require that you imagine you are interviewing with a specific company—perhaps one of your Lead Is?

Write only phrases in answer to the questions. You do not need to write complete sentences and memorize them. You are trying to be genuine, not rehearsed.

If the question requires a yes or no answer, *always* move beyond that one-word answer with an explanation: *Yes, I believe that arriving on time is an excellent indicator of timeliness and attention to detail.*

Brainstorm good answers with friends or classmates.

Look over the questions and your answers *before each* interview.

1. Tell me about yourself.

2. What are some of your strengths? (Variation: Why should we hire you?) (See section that follows on page 206: Proving a Strength.)

3. What are some of your weaknesses? (What is your biggest challenge?) (See section that follows on page 209: Flipping a Negative to a Positive.)

4. Why do you want to work here? (Variation: Why do you want this job?)

5. How long would you stay with us if this job were offered to you?

6. What can you offer us that someone else cannot? (Variation: What is unique about you?)

7. What did you like least about your last job? (Remember to frame in the positive.)

8. Why did you leave your last job (rather than "I hated the boss," how about, "A more creative opportunity came up"?)

9. What is your opinion of the organization you are currently working for? (Always emphasize the positive aspects.)

10. What about the position under discussion interests you the least? The most?

11. What preparation have you had for the position?

12. Are you willing to do shift work? *(Especially applicable in software, publishing, culinary, and retail positions.)*

13. Why do you like the kind of work for which you are applying?

Those are a success who have lived well, laughed often and loved much; who have gained the respect of intelligent people and the love of children; who have filled their niche and accomplished their task; who leave the world better than they found it, whether by a perfect poem or a rescued soul; who never lacked appreciation of the earth's beauty or failed to express it; who looked for the best in others and gave the best they had.
—Ralph Waldo Emerson

14. What kind of boss or leader do you prefer to work for?

15. What do you know about our organization? *(You can choose one of your leads for this — emphasize the positive.)*

16. May I contact your previous employers?

17. Do you find this type of work satisfying?

18. Would you choose this same line of work or major again? Why?

19. Are you willing to leave this area if you are transferred to another branch of our organization?

20. How did you find out about this position?

21. Describe an accomplishment of which you are particularly proud.

22. What was the best thing about your educational program?

23. What personal attributes do you feel are necessary to succeed in this field?

24. Describe your ideal job after graduation.

25. Do you plan to continue your education?

26. What does success mean to you?

27. What project have you done which relates to this position?

28. Describe what you learned in your student internship. *(If you haven't done an internship, use an example from a job you've had—don't give up the opportunity to tell them you are a quick learner and internalize lessons learned.)*

29. Tell me about your educational program.

30. Do you think your GPA is a good indicator of your academic or artistic ability? (*Mention here how proud you are of working and maintaining a good academic record, or how your grades have improved.*)

31. In what community and/or school activities have you been involved?

32. What are your long range career goals?

33. Are you willing to work overtime? (Especially applicable in any software, gaming, start-up, or growing company.)

34. How has your schooling prepared you for this job?

35. How do you think a friend or teacher who knows you well would describe you?

36. If you were a _____ (*cereal, tree, bird, other animal options*) what would you be? Why?

37. How have you changed during your schooling?

38. Why did you choose your particular field?

39. Do you arrive at work or school on time?

40. What do you think determines a person's progress in a good company?

41. What do you do to handle criticism?

42. What have you learned from some of the jobs you've held?

43. What interests you about our product or service?

44. Which of your college years was the most difficult?

45. Define teamwork.

46. What do you think is a realistic 3 year plan for yourself?

47. Describe your artistic work methods.

48. What decisions are easiest for you to make? The hardest?

49. What is the most important decision that you would make differently if you were to make it again?

50. How would your instructors describe your recent standards of performance?

51. Describe your relationship with your last supervisor (or portfolio or senior seminar instructor).

52. What kind of supervisor gets the best performance out of you?

53. Describe one or two inspired moments of which you're particularly proud.

54. When you are given a creative assignment, what is your method of solution, your process?

55. How many hours a day should a person spend on his/her job?

56. What do you feel is an acceptable attendance record?

57. What do you see yourself doing professionally in 10 years?

58. What is unique about you? (Variation: What can you bring to this job that someone else cannot?)

59. If you could spend time doing what you really love to do, what would that be?

60. What have you done to create a path toward your goals?

61. What is your strategy for meeting deadlines?

62. Describe your perfect workplace.

63. If you have to divide your daily life into 3 parts, what would those parts be?

64. Do you plan to continue going to school throughout your life?

65. What is your strategy for staying on top of revolutionary technology?

66. Describe your perfect client or employer.

67. Tell us about a significant failure and what you learned from it. Has it changed your behavior?

68. What extracurricular activities have you participated in while you've been in school?

69. What are some of the challenges you are facing in your current job and what are you doing to overcome them?

70. What type of tasks do you enjoy doing most?

71. What do you think it takes to succeed in your industry today?

72. What kind of skills do you bring to group or team projects?

73. When have you done the best work you are capable of?

74. What are some of the most significant things you have learned from your educational program?

75. How do you handle conflict with your peers?

76. What kind of people do you like to work with best?

77. How would you describe your attitude toward risk in industry or business or career terms?

78. What trends do you see in your field?

79. Tell us about a time when you were creative in solving a problem.

80. Tell us about a time when you had to adapt to a difficult situation.

81. What is your best technical skill?

82. Which technical skill will you focus on improving?

83. What is your best creative skill?

84. Why should we hire you?

85. What salary would you expect? (**Never** *name a figure — use the term "market rates" or "I'm willing to negotiate on the salary." Be sure you know what the going rate is! Ask for the typical hourly or day rate at your professional organization — AIGA, IDSA, ASID, AIA, IICS, etc.)*

Others you have encountered:

One of the most common interview questions is: **Tell <u>me</u> <u>a</u>bout <u>y</u>ourself.** It even has an acronym: TMAY (pronounced T-MAY). How do you go about preparing for this *quick, short, **punchy** introduction* without sounding like your mom, your very strange Uncle Billy, or an egomaniac?

Your résumé and portfolio are the ***foundation*** for all parts of your interview, including the typical interview questions. **You** are in control of the information you give out about yourself. In other words, you *manage* the information for "your corporation." Think about your answer to the TMAY question as a **mission statement** for your corporation.

Pick up your résumé and check for the following information:

- portfolio skills necessary for this job (remember, you've done your research)
- personal skills useful for this job (team work, skilled leader and follower, etc.)
- education (focus on the positive always)
- experience useful for this job
- honors and achievements

And add:

- general, positive goals
- your values as they apply to business

Avoid mentioning:

- personal difficulties and problems you've overcome
- negatives about school or people you know
- generalizations about groups of people or "the government,"
- or a deep analysis of your childhood

Tips

- Remain positive.
- Focus on the *best* in you.
- Express enthusiasm, which is what employers look for *first* in an employee, but don't gush (leave your pom-poms at home).

Method:

1. **Think of a "catchy" first line** that says something about you. For instance:

   - I'm a big city girl from a small town.

   - I've always wanted to be Giupetto and make my characters come to life.

   - My life was changed when I saw _____, and I wanted to create magical stories to change people's lives.

   - I come from a long line of creative people.

   - I was three when I started playing my own compositions.

   - My sister dragged me to guitar lessons. That guitar made all the difference in my life.

   - I was born to draw. I can't remember when I haven't been drawing characters.

   - I'm from the lentil capital of the world.

   - I grew up in the middle of orange groves near a small college town.

   - **YOU think of your own. Design it!**

2. Having developed a nifty first line, do not dwell on your childhood. Move directly to your professional preparation or professional career.

It's important for you to **write a rough draft**. Read the rough draft ***out loud*** to yourself *several times*. Change the **final draft** to reflect how you actually speak.

Use complete sentence form for this exercise. When you are preparing for an interview, *bullet the points you want to make,* but **don't memorize the entire speech** since it is too easy to forget a line and then be totally lost. Soon, you will be able to "roll the tape" of your introduction without a hitch.

Here's my *rough draft*. This is how I *write*, not how I *speak*. The sentences are so complex that I'd never be able to create a flowing verbal delivery.

I've realized a childhood dream. I'm about to graduate from College of Art and Industry with a major in the Arts of Animation. I've discovered that there are more applications for my design and computer skills than I realized. Working part time while I was in college helped me develop time management skills and budgeting skills, and shift management afforded me a leadership experience as well. My grades have steadily improved while I've been in school, and last quarter I was named to the Dean's List.

I value timeliness, a solid work ethic, yet appreciate a balanced approach to work and health.

I have an optimistic view of the world, see problems as challenges to my creativity, and I like working with a team to arrive at rich solutions. My particular skill is figuring out the steps to seeing solutions through to achievement.

The soundbite above is too wordy and overly complicated. It reflects how I **write**, not how I actually speak.

So, here's my **Final Draft:**

I've dreamed about being an animator since I was a kid in an Iowa cornfield . I'm about to graduate from the College of Art and Industry in the Arts of Animation. I've found out I can do more with animations than I imagined and that thrills me.

I've worked part-time while I've been going to school, and I've really gotten good at juggling school, work, and a sliver of a personal life. In my last job, I was given some management responsibility as well as creative and production work, and I really liked helping my team do well. My grades have gotten better as I've become more organized, and last quarter I was named to the Dean's List.

I'm optimistic; I love creative challenges; and I am passionate about my work.

See the difference between the rough draft and the final draft?

Your turn

Things you want to include: list at least 5.

1.   4.
2.   5.
3.   6.

Your first sentence (punchy but not cocky…)

_____

_____

Add it to your first draft:

_____
_____
_____
_____
_____
_____
_____
_____
_____
_____
_____

Edit for personality, continuity, and clarity.

- Check for positive outlook.

- Read it out loud 5 times.

- Edit the parts your tongue stumbles over or that sound stilted read aloud.

Your final draft:

_____
_____
_____
_____
_____
_____
_____
_____
_____
_____
_____

Shortened versions of your soundbite are *great* for networking situations, parties, and meeting new people in any situation.

Your shortened (5 – 6 lines) bulleted version is? Memorize only the *keywords*. They'll guide you in your presentation of your TMAY.

_____

_____

_____

_____

_____

_____

One more thing (or two...)
- Practice a *genuine* smile.
- Practice looking directly into the eyes of the person you're being introduced to.
- Practice interest in the other person (a sure cure for shyness).
- Practice a firm handshake.
- Practice introducing yourself (first **and** last name — you're a professional creative now).
- You'll be terrific!

It is common to be asked in an interview about **your strengths.** Honestly assessing what you're good at in terms of *technical or traditional skills, personal skills, digital skills, and organizational and conceptual skills* is the mark of maturity and of a professional.

The *employer/client will want to know* what it is that **you** bring to the marketplace and *how you'll benefit his/her business.* It's your job to identify what those benefits are and how they can be an aid to a particular company. We'll explore *how to*

- identify your strengths,
- demonstrate the strengths with an anecdote (story),
- apply the strengths to the job at hand, and
- prove you and your skills will be an asset to the company.

It is also common to be asked what **weaknesses or challenges** you have. You'll focus on a weakness, deficit, or challenge you have identified on your résumé.

- Little experience in your field?
- Job hopping to accommodate your schedule?
- AA or AAA rather than a BA?

You'll *acknowledge the interviewer's perceptive ability* to see what is missing. You'll *demonstrate your acquisition of the strength; prove it with an anecdote*; and *apply the skill to the client's or employer's business.*

Both strengths and weaknesses are based on your résumé. **Keep these topics on a professional level** as *demonstrated by your résumé.* This is not the place to confess embarrassing little personal tidbits you see as weaknesses. ***Keep it professional.***

The deep things of personal experience make us know that a man's life is not any sort of intellectual puzzle to be ferreted out but a gift to be received and a task to be fulfilled.
—Nathan A. Scott

Proving a strength and *flipping a weakness to a strength* and then proving that strength *have much in common.* Here are the steps in both:

Proving a strength

1. State strength
2. Tell a story (anecdote) in which strength is demonstrated
3. Apply strength to the job and/or client in question

Flipping a weakness to a strength and proving it

1. Acknowledge the interviewer's perception
2. Find the strength perceived to be missing (flip to strength)
3. Tell a story in which strength is demonstrated
4. Apply strength to the job and/or client in question

A word of caution

In the last decade, political public relations people have learned to put a *positive spin* on almost any action. They've been called *spin doctors,* a rather negative descriptor. *Your task* is to *remain genuine* yet *positive*, rather than cynical and spinning when you are changing a perceived into a strength.

Proving a Strength

State what your most prominent strength is.

- You may choose from the list that follows, from your résumé, or come up with one of your own.

- This strength **should also appear on your résumé** in one of the Skills categories. If a strength comes to mind that is not on your résumé, put   it there!

- Make sure this is *genuinely* part of your personality, conceptual, digital, or traditional skills.

- You'll need to *prove it by telling a short story that demonstrates this strength in action,* and finally demonstrate *how this strength can be applied to the job/client in question.*

Here are some personal strengths for you to consider (Make sure the strengths you identify are on your résumé.):

fast learner	dependability	leadership
analytical ability	enthusiasm	ability to take risks
perseverance	resourcefulness	speaking skills
writing skills	loyalty	dedication
thoroughness	practical approach	punctuality
good listening skills	self-motivation	problem solver
common sense	detail oriented	troubleshooter
communication skills	team player	patience
persuasiveness	innovative ideas	assertiveness
ability to handle pressure	maturity	follow through
hard worker	good grades	outgoing

Other categories of strengths might apply to software, design, or fabrication skills you've acquired — check the "Skills" section of your résumé. So, perhaps your strength is that you thoroughly understand principles of (can apply, demonstrate, and/or teach):

game design	cartooning	Director®
layout	3D modeling	HTML
MS software	Softimage®	Adobe software

others programs and/or platforms:

_____   _____   _____

_____   _____   _____

Other strengths:

_____

_____

_____

_____

Steps in *proving a strength:*

1. **Name your strength**.

   You might say: *I've really had fun working with Photoshop® and have gotten pretty good at it.*

2. **Prove a strength:** Tell a story about a time when this particular skill was demonstrated.

   - Where were you?
   - What was the problem?
   - How did your skill solve the problem?

You might say: *When I was in the computer lab, I ended up helping several students work through difficulties in Photoshop® assignments.   I not only enhanced my Photoshop® skills, but had fun troubleshooting tool.*

3. **Apply to the job or client:** Tell us how your skill can help a business or a client. Apply the skill to the job in question. How can this strength or skill be an asset to a business?

   You might say: *On the job, I can use Photoshop® as a tool to quickly implement design ideas as well as help troubleshoot other computer applications for timely output.*

Now, it's your turn:
   1. Your strength is: _____
   _____

   2. An anecdote (short illustrative story) in which your strength was demonstrated:

   _____
   _____
   _____

   _____

   _____

   _____

   3. Demonstrate how that strength can be an asset to the employer/client's business.

   _____
   _____

   _____

Good for you!

Acknowledging a Liability, Deficit or a Challenge in your résumé (changing a perceived negative into a positive).

What is your greatest weakness (or biggest challenge)? is a very common interview question.

1. Recognize the interviewer's concern as a *legitimate issue* (job hopping, lack of experience, age—too young or too mature [overqualified], grades are some common concerns).

   - What you're doing here is honoring another's perception.

   - It also helps to lower your natural defensive posture and really think about what might be an asset to your own corporation.

   Scenario A. You might say: *"I understand that you may feel that I've changed jobs quite a bit while I was in school."*

   Scenario B. You can also choose a liability which is also a strength: *I am a demon for completion and will do **anything** to see a job through.*

2. Identify the strength that is perceived by the interviewer as missing (the weakness is the opposite side of the coin of a strength).

   Scenario A. You might continue: *"You may see that as lacking perseverance, but I see it as **creative flexibility** to accommodate a quarterly change in schedule."*

   - Now that I've named the strength (creative flexibility), I get to work it into the conversation in various ways—watch for it in Scenario A.

   Scenario B. You might say: *"I need to remind myself to **positively** direct others who are not as dedicated to a professional end   product, and have been attending seminars in leadership techniques.*

No whines or excuses here. Just state the strength.

3. Use an example or an anecdote to prove the underlying strength that the interviewer perceives as missing.

> **Scenario A.** You might continue: *"As my schedule changed each quarter, I approached my employer to work within his/her needs and still complete my degree. In many cases, we reached a satisfactory solution."*

> **Scenario B.** *"I've found I can get people to produce quicker and more creatively with positive direction and reinforcement. When I was team captain on my last project we came in on time and under budget for a very satisfied client."*

4. Identify how that strength might *apply to the job* you are interviewing for.

> **Scenario A.** You might conclude:
> *"Many businesses attempt to deal with conflicting client needs. I believe my skills at being **creatively flexible** developed while I was in school and working at the same time would be an asset in satisfactorily accommodating the client while remaining true to your business needs."*

> **Scenario B.** *"I'm a positive motivator and skilled team leader, and work to enhance a smoothly functioning creative group."*

Now, it's your turn.

1. Name the weakness or challenge in your résumé or skills:

_____

_____

2. Acknowledge the weakness in your résumé:

   Start with: *"I understand that you might see _____ as a weakness in my résumé."*

   or: *"You may want to discuss _____."*

3. What strength is the flip side of the weakness? (If you've changed jobs many times, persistence is perceived as missing; so, the flip side of that weakness might be flexibility, which is a strength.)

   _____

4. **Tell us a story** in which the strength (perceived as missing) is demonstrated:

   _____
   _____
   _____
   _____
   _____
   _____
   _____
   _____

5. How could you **apply that strength** you've just revealed to the client/job you're imagining? How would you become an asset?

   _____
   _____
   _____

A Note:

Most of us have a disability of one sort or another. You don't? Perhaps you haven't found it yet! Some are more apparent than others, and some have to deal with theirs daily. *Acknowledge your disability if it will show up on the job.* Then prove how you've overcome it or learned to work with it in the same way as above, so that *what others perceive as a liability is really an asset.*

For instance: dyslexic?

> *I've learned to work with my dyslexia. In fact, it is because of it that I've become so good with images. I carry a spell checker with me and use it always, and I enlist an ally to proof my graphic work. I, in turn, help with the impact of images. Images have been my primary means of communication since I was small. It is this understanding of the impact of different styles as well as the creation of images that would be an asset to your business.*

*Resource built upon: John L. LeFevre, *How You Really Get Hired,* p. 91-105. See Resource List included in the Addenda of this book.

212

```
┌··············································┐
:                    Illegal and             :
:         Inappropriate Questions            :
└··············································┘
```

You can't depend on your eyes when your imagination is out of focus. —Mark Twain

Questions which relate to your *ethnic origin, religion, gender, financial status, marital status, handicap, or age* are illegal **to ask** as they cannot be used to discriminate among job applicants in the United States.

Additionally, questions about *sexual preference* may be illegal as well. Protection from discrimination on the basis of sexual orientation varies from state to state (generally, states on either the East or the West coast are more liberal). Check your state.

The statutes which cover discrimination in employment include:

Title VII of the Civil Rights Act of 1964, which requires that consideration for employment **may not be based** in any way on ethnicity, gender, religion, or national origin. Title VII is enforced by the Equal Employment Opportunity Commission (EEOC), established in 1965.

Since 1979, EEOC has also been responsible for enforcing:

- Age Discrimination in Employment Act (ADEA), which prohibits discrimination based on age, protecting workers aged 40 to 70. The dot-coms have been particularly vulnerable on this issue.

- Equal Pay Act (EPA) of 1963, aimed at leveling pay for both genders performing *substantially* equal work. This is still an issue in the contemporary workplace.

- Section 501 of the Rehabilitation Act of 1973, as amended, protects employment opportunities for citizens with a handicap.

- Title VII, as amended in 1978 included the Pregnancy Discrimination Act, in which pregnancy is considered a medical condition and falls under medical issues in employment policy.

- Title VII, as amended in 1981 defines sexual harassment (one's ability to *obtain, retain, or advance* in employment is linked to giving sexual favors) and prohibits it in the workplace. This law has been the subject of recent controversy ("one free hit," no matter how lewd, has been the issue). Since it is a controversial issue, it will probably be the subject of litigation and may change in your working lifetime.

Title VII applies to organizations *having 15 or more employees*, including private employers, state and local governments, educational institutions and labor organizations. The number of employees restriction has been the subject of recent litigation, and this law, too, may change in your working lifetime.

If you feel your rights have been violated, phone the Equal Employment Opportunity Commission in your state. *Be aware that you must have **proof** to succeed in your complaint.*

It is common that within six months of entering the workplace, you will become an initial interviewer. As an *interviewer*, you, too, must obey the law. You would not want to jeopardize your position or your corporation by inviting a lawsuit. Ignorance is not a defense, so it is up to you to study your company's guidelines regarding interviewing.

Generally, **what is legal or appropriate and what is not?**

Job related questions are appropriate.

If you have to be 18 years old to operate machinery or 21 years old to tend bar legally, it is appropriate and legal to ask you *if you are older than* 18 or 21 years old. (**Not**, *how old are you?*)

*Title VII resource built upon: How to Win the Job You Really Want, by Janice Weinberg, pp. 154 – 156. See Resource List included in the Addenda.

If you have to lift 150 lbs. on the job, then it is appropriate to ask for a demonstration. But if lifting 150 lbs. is not a part of the job, then asking for a demonstration of such a strength is discriminatory.

Non-job-related questions are **inappropriate.** (Example: Are you single?)

You have a choice whether to answer or to *politely* deflect the question. (Of course! You may choose to answer these questions if you wish to.) **It is the asking**, *not the answering*, that is questionable. The *interviewer may try to rattle you* with questions which are not illegal, but are inappropriate, to see how you handle difficult situations.

Practice two or three good (and polite) deflections for inappropriate questions.

Approaches

 There are at least **three** good non-confrontational, non-committal, but genuine **approaches** to take:

1. **The Query** (with a puzzled look on your face):

   - *"I'm sorry. I don't understand how this question relates to the job at hand. Would you please explain?"* (Smile)
   - *"I'm not sure I understand the question. Could you clarify?"*

2. **The Light Approach**:

   - *"No kidding? You have to be single (or have a certain reading list, or go to a certain church, etc.) to take this job?"*

   - *"Wow! Mom and Pop are going to be on the job with me?"*

   - The Light Approach must be handled delicately, taking care not to sound like a smart-aleck or too cocky. Not everyone's sense of humor is similar to yours.

3. **The Redirect:**

   - *"Let me show you my favorite piece from my portfolio."*

   - *"Perhaps you can tell me about what you'd like to see accomplished in this job."* Here is the opportunity to use one of the questions you've prepared to ask in the interview.

   - *"Let me show you how a recent trip inspired a new direction in my work."* You take out a small piece not included in your portfolio showing.

Here are a few inappropriate or illegal questions you may encounter.

Try to think of the underlying illegal or inappropriate reason for the question. Try to think *when (or if!)* it would be appropriate to *ask* any of these questions if you were the interviewer.

Pick at least 5 to answer. Answer each 3 ways:
- with The Query
- with The Light Approach
- with The Redirect

Give at least one answer to each question. Write phrases, not complete sentences, for reminders to study *before* your interviews. Remember, keep it *genuine but respectful*.

1. Have you received any speeding tickets in the last 12 months?

2. How do you spend your Sundays?

3. Do you provide entertainment in your home very often?

4. Do you have a girlfriend/boyfriend?

5. Do you enjoy the opposite sex?

6. Do you have any personal debts?

7. Are you from a dysfunctional family?

8. Do you have any mental, emotional, or physical disabilities?

9. Which church do you attend?

10. Are there any religious holidays you observe that would prevent you from doing your work?

Disorder is always in a hurry.
—Napoleon

11. What kind of books/movies do you enjoy?

12. Do you drink? (*response should be non-alcohol related*)

13. Which one of your parents had the most profound influence on your overall development?

14. What was your home life like?

15. What is your marital status?

16. Were you ever divorced?

17. Do you have any savings?

18. Have you ever had your wages garnished (or garnisheed)?

19. Have you ever applied for credit and been refused?

20. What are your mother's and father's educational backgrounds and occupations?

21. Where do your ancestors come from?

22. Would you show us your birth certificate **before** we decide to hire you?

23. Have you ever had a criminal record **for which a pardon has been granted**?

24. Were you ever arrested?

25. How old are you?

26. Are you pregnant?

27. Are you planning to have any children?

28. Do you have any dependents?

29. Why did you leave school?

30. How did you support yourself while going to school?

31. How do you feel about school prayer?

32. What political party do you belong to?

33. Are you single?

34. Some friends and I are going salmon fishing this weekend. Would you like to join us?

    Hint: male or female, you answer should be, *"Thank you for thinking of me, but I already have other plans."* Interviews are **not** social situations.

35. Others you've encountered and good answers:

    _____
    _____
    _____
    _____
    _____
    _____
    _____
    _____

Other considerations
You may be asked if, after employment, you can submit legal documentation to allow you to work in the United States.

- You do not have to submit them until *after* the offer of employment is tendered.

- Employers in the United States are fined if they hire people who do not have such documents.

- Sometimes an employment application will ask you to forego the right to wait until after the offer of employment is made to show documents that prove your eligibility to work in the US—read the fine print carefully.

It is *never* appropriate to use interviewing as an opportunity to set up a date, and *your answer to an invitation issued in an interview (#34 above) should always be:*

"Thank you for thinking of me, but I already have plans."

You *cannot assume* that this situation features a man asking a woman for a date at an interview, nor can you assume that this is an attraction of the opposite sex. In today's world, the person in the superior position may be female or male. Chauvinism and inappropriate behavior are *not* gender specific.

Privacy of information given and/or the right to ask certain questions *varies from state to state* and is dealt with exhaustively in *Your Rights in the Workplace* by Barbara K. Repa. See *Resource List* included in the Addenda of this book.

Employment Application

Employment applications *vary from state to state* since they are legal documents, but you should be prepared to answer some questions common to most employment applications.

Bring with you information which will aid you in filling out an application.

- References
- Résumé
- Addresses of former employment
- Years of graduation from various levels of school
- Social Security card
- A blue pen and a black pen
  - in case at the end of the application, it specifies which color pen
  - *lately a blue pen has been used for original documents* since photocoping makes all words on documents black.

Be thorough in filling in the application in your best and most legible writing or professional printing.

Fill in *all* the blanks.

For the blank which asks *salary desired*, put *market rates* (or *negotiable*) and of course, find out from your local professional organization what market rates are! Salaries for jobs are different in different parts of the country, depending on supply and demand, as well as on cost of living. Once you have named a figure for salary desired, you are committed to that salary and should accept if it is offered.

Authorizations

You may be asked the following on an employment application: Is all the information truthful? Be sure it is, as any deceit is grounds for instant dismissal. This can mean leaving things out as well (omission).

In the middle of difficulty lies opportunity. —Albert Einstein

You may have to agree to a medical and/or drug test on a continuing basis, at random and at the company's will within the law with the results disclosed to the employer. **Read the application carefully before you sign it.**

As mentioned before, what happens to physical samples once testing has been completed is a recent legal issue under Title VII of the 1964 Civil Rights Act.   If you fail a drug test, your chances of being hired by this company are slim—very, very slim. (Since recent grads who have been recreational drug users are particularly vulnerable at graduation, why don't you help out your classmates by upholding their resolve to stay clean?)

If you have a false positive (possibly 5% of drug tests), by all means, *ask for another test*. Some substances that give false positives?

- second-hand marijuana smoke (marijuana, of course)
- poppy seeds (opiates)
- ibuprophen (marijuana)
- a cold medicine to help you sleep at night (opiates)
- a prescription for Valium (Angel Dust)

You may have to authorize the company to investigate the information you've supplied.

You may be asked to provide:
- proof of identity
- citizenship
- work permit (Green Card)
- driver's license
- Social Security card

The employment application is a legal document.

- ***Read it carefully!***

- If you have any questions, **be sure to ask for clarification.**

- *Not knowing* or *not clearly understanding* is **not** a defense in the business world, so be sure to *ask* if you have questions, *before* you sign the document.

*Resource on drug tests: *Knock 'Em Dead 1999*, p. 237–238 by Martin John Yate. See Resouce List included in the Addenda.

Employment Application

Personal Information   Social Security Number _____
Full name (First, MI, Last): _____
Present address: _____
Permanent address: _____
Phone number: _____ E-mail _____
Referred by: _____ Are you 18 years old or older ? Y N

Employment Desired
Position _____
Date you can start _____ Salary desired _____
Are you employed now? _____
May we inquire of your present employer? _____
Ever applied to this company before? Y N   When? _____ Where? _____

Education	**Name & Location**	**Yrs. completed**	**Grad?**	**Subj/Degree?**
Elementary				
High School				
College				
Trade School or Licensing School				

Former Employers (last one first)

Date	Name	Address	Position	Salary	Left because?
1.					
2.					
3.					
4.					

References
1. _____
2. _____

Signed: _____ Date: _____

The Interview: A Checklist

Check off your interview preparedness.

Preparation

_____ Research company
- products
- clients
- names of principals
- human resources director
- list of questions to be asked by you
- review answers to possible interview questions

_____ Call for appointment
- confirm the day before with a phone call

_____ Appearance as representative of your corporation and as potential employee of this company

Check:
- pierces out except ears
- tattoos covered
- hemline
- smile
- clothing for smoke, other odors
- nails/hands clean
- scent (wear none)
- shoes shined
- pantyhose (take extra pair)

_____ Pen — take two! (one blue—many legal documents have you sign in blue since black is the color of copies, one black)

_____ Location of interview
- Do you know how to get there?
- How long will it take?

No one can make you feel inferior without your consent.
—Eleanor Roosevelt

Interview

_____ Timeliness
- be at least 5 minutes early
- plan how you're going to get there
- there is **no** good excuse for being late

_____ Do not drink or smoke before, during, or after interview

_____ Attitude

_____ Eye-contact, handshake, body posture

_____ Listening skills

_____ Careful but genuine answers to questions: review

_____ Paperwork: Have *extra copies* of

- your résumé
- color Sample Sheet
- references
- letters of recommendation
- business cards

_____ Take list of names, addresses, and phone number of your former employers and references so you'll be ready to fill in employment application

Yes, you'll be asked to fill in information, even if you have a résumé.

_____ Portfolio: organized and ready for presentation

- Take no work you have to apologize for
- Take *only first-rate work*
- You don't have any work which looks like this company's work? **Do some!** *Your competition will*.

- Order your portfolio so that pieces the company will be interested in (work like they do...) are in front, the others after that so if you don't get to them or time runs out, it won't be a disaster.

- If you are keen on saving your best work for last for maximum impact, have that piece represented on your Sample Sheet, so if the interview is shortened, your best piece will still have been presented.

Afterward

_____ Follow-up:
    _____ thank you letter(s)
    _____ self-promotional flyers, newsletters, etc.
    _____ post card of your work
    _____ short note with Sample Sheet of new work
    _____ periodic updates with your work shown on the front

Relax. You'll find just the right spot for you. You are ready!

Make sure your appearance reflects your attention to detail and overall approach to your professional life.

Congratulations! You've received an offer. Don't be surprised! You've worked hard for this. Your portfolio is terrific. You look good. You're well rehearsed. You've *already researched* the following before you applied for the job (you have, haven't you?!):

- place of the company in the marketplace,
- its competitors,
- its strategies,
- years in business,
- number of employees,
- recent mass turnover, etc.

There are *some* remaining considerations for you to give some thought to before you accept.

- *Compensation package* (wages and benefits, detailed in the following section).
- *Negotiation strategies.*

And some of the following *issues to decide* whether to accept the offer. It's important to develop your own checklist, but here are some suggestions:

- Will you *enjoy* the *daily tasks* of the position?

- Does the job present *continuing challenges*?

- Is this a *team* you can *work* with comfortably?

- Are there *extraordinary time considerations*?
  - overtime?
  - lots of out-of-town travel?
  - commuting time?
  - seasonal peaks which require a great deal of overtime or layoffs?

If at first you do succeed—try to hide your astonishment.
—Harry F. Banks

- Is the *corporate culture* one in which you will thrive? (pressure, formality, politics, etc.)?

- Is the *working environment* physically safe?

- Are there *long-range goals* with which you can identify?

- Will you be expected *to move continuously*?

- Others:_____

  _____
  _____
  _____
  _____

Sometimes it helps to establish a plus **(+)** column and a minus **(-)** column to weigh your response to the offer.

+	-
1.	
2.	
3.	
4.	
5.	
6.	

The Offer

An *offer* comes *after these criteria are met*:

- the company fits your *needs, values, ideals*
- your *portfolio* shows you are a terrific designer or artist
- the *chemistry* is right (remember, this is a two-way street)
- you like the team members and company atmosphere, and
- they like you.

So, once you have been through the interview *process*, and have been back *several times* to meet many of your potential team members, *it is likely that you will be offered a position*.

Once you've been offered a position, **salary and benefits will be discussed.**

Salary and benefits are called a *compensation package.* When there are *more jobs* available than workers to fill them, this package is *more* inclusive. When there are *more workers* than jobs available, then the package is *less* inclusive.

While a salary or wages may have *a range* from which the offer will come, the rest of the compensation package, even at the lower levels of jobs, *can be negotiated.* Any experience you have increases the opportunity for negotiation, so get that freelance or part time industry job **now**.

Salary is a *yearly* wage, divided up into twelve or twenty-four parts.

- Managerial, design, creative, and supervisory work is often paid in salary.

- Rarely is there overtime paid, but you are expected to work until the job is done—no matter how long it takes. You are paid the same if you work a few hours or many hours.

Wages are *hourly* compensation.

- Technical work often is paid in wages.

- Overtime is paid for those who work more than 40 hours per week.

- Union jobs are often paid in wages as negotiated by a union contract.

Contract work is often paid in a lump sum for duration of the contract, or a salary for the duration of the contract (it may be stated in yearly terms, but **do not assume that a year is the length of the contract).**

A compensation package includes the following:

- salary (yearly wages) or wages (hourly) (often a range, negotiable within that range)

- paid overtime (only if you are an hourly worker, usually none if you are on salary)

- benefits (negotiable inclusion and percentages paid by the company)

- who is included in various insurance policies (dependents, domestic partner, spouse, elders)

  - life
  - health
  - dental
  - vision

- leaves for elder care (beyond legal requirements)

- help with child care

- maternity, paternity, and newborn leave (beyond legal requirements)

- transportation passes and parking permits

- paid moving costs for relocation

- paid sick days

- paid health club fees

- company festivities

- retirement or 401 K investment plan (vesting times possibly negotiable)

Take a *deep breath* **before accepting** and **consider the following.**

Things *to avoid*:

- *accepting immediately unless* it is exactly the wage/salary and compensation package you have already stated you will accept.

- (Make sure *on application form* to write "market rates" (and then know what they are!) or "negotiable."

- accepting without considering what the offer means to you in terms of your *goals, values, and ideals.*

- accepting without considering if this compensation package will meet your needs in terms of financial obligations.

- accepting without getting *each item* in the compensation package *clearly defined.*

Things *to know*:

Salaries have a **RANGE.** There is a:

- high end
- middle range
- lower end

The high end is what CEO's are paid—*mucho dinero.*
The middle range is what middle management is paid.
The lower range is what workers are paid.

Each range will have levels—for instance:

- upper level of the low range,
- the middle level of the low range
- and the lower level of the low range.

Your ***first offer*** *will come from the lower part of the lower range* for an entry level job.

You will want to negotiate that offer up to the middle or upper part of the low range. That's why you got that internship, isn't it? Not only for valuable experience, but for negotiating power. You didn't get an internship? *Get one now.* (Even a couple of hours a week will help your negotiating power.)

Always ask for some *clearly defined time* to think the offer over.

- You might say: *I'm very enthusiastic about the opportunity to work with the team I've met. I'd like some time to think it through. May I call you on Tuesday at 8:30 to discuss your offer?*

The ball is now in your court. The company has invested quite a bit of time in selecting its candidate. Keep in mind that *time = money.*

The participants in the company want you to like them and their offer so they don't have to invest more time and more effort in finding another candidate.

The employer might be a bit surprised that you'd be willing to negotiate, since so few newly graduated candidates understand the power they have and that they will never be cheaper and are highly trained. Make sure your negotiated suggestions are polite, reasonable, and market driven.

Get the offer in writing. (Many companies make written offers as a matter of course.)

- List all the terms of the compensation package mentioned on a piece of paper you've brought, and then ask for confirmation as you restate each item.

- Ask for an initial on the paper on which you've listed each item.

- *Will an employer* promise something and then *become forgetful* and not follow through? *You bet*! It may not be intentional, but it's a good idea to protect yourself and clarify the offer.

- You might say: *Just so I'm clear about your offer, may I read back the items to you?*

- After you've read them through: *Could I ask you to initial the list? Thank you. Would you like a copy?*

- Ask the office manager to make a copy. *You keep the original.*

- Now you can take the time to figure out if your expenses can be made to match the offer. How about the cost of moving, your student loans, transportation to work, etc.?

Take time to consider what is best for you in the short and long term, given your values, goals, and ideals.

- You've done your financial planning, so you can figure out what you'll need in financial compensation.

- You've *already researched what a similar position pays in this town* (by calling your local professional association).

- Now, you're armed with two pieces of information:

  1. what you'll need to cover your financial obligations

  2. what is typically paid for this position (or type of work)

You are ready to learn the rules of negotiation.

The two most commonly used types of negotiation are: ***Hardball*** and ***Win-Win.*

Hardball is a type of negotiation in which:

- There is a clear winner and clear loser.
- You try to wear the other person down or defeat him/her.
- This is Vince Lombardi's type of winning: *"Winning isn't everything, it's the only thing."*

The *upside* of hardball:
- It's short term.
- When it's done, it's done.

The *downside* of hardball:
- You always have to be alert for the retaliation of a fallen adversary.
- You have to "watch your back."
- You lose a potential ally.

The rules of Hardball:

1. Take the initiative. Make an outrageous offer; your adversary might be unwary and take it.

2. Be prepared to walk away.

3. Don't make threats unless you're prepared to back them up.

4. Understand your opponent's weaknesses and vulnerabilities and be prepared to expose and use them. Squeeze hard.

5. Understand your opponent's goals and motivations so you can see through the smoke screen of rhetoric.

6. Always ask for more than you want, so you have a fall-back position.

7. Create a demand by starting a bidding war.

8. Get your adversary to say "yes" as often as possible (the Used Car Sales technique).

9. You don't have to settle for less than you want. Hold firm. Wear 'em down.

10. Take no prisoners.

Win-Win is a type of negotiation in which creative compromise is used so that each side gives and each side receives benefit.

The *upside* of Win-Win:

- Both parties come away at least partially satisfied.
- Both parties are willing to work together in the future.
- There is potential for future creative compromise.

The *downside* of Win-Win:

- It takes time.
- There is no one clearly defined winner.
- Both partners must be open to the possibilities.

The rules of Win-Win:

1. Long term relationships are the goal.

2. Consider no other option but for both parties to benefit.

3. Be prepared. Do your research for positions relative to your own.

4. View the other party as a partner in a creative compromise.

5. *Listen.* Ask questions. Really listen to what is being said and what underlies what is being said.

6. Consider flexible solutions rather than set solutions.

7. State what you want clearly and show how the other party can help you get what you want.

8. View compromise as creative solution, not loss. Keep the "greater good" in mind.

9. See conflict as opportunity, and problems as challenges to your creativity and ingenuity.

10. If you really cannot come up with a mutually satisfying solution, part company on pleasant terms so that you can have the opportunity to do business together in the future.

11. The spirit of win-win negotiation is that both parties benefit, and both come back to do business with each other again.

Now that you know the rules, you are ready to negotiate.

You've been *offered a job* with a certain compensation package.

- You've *asked for some time to consider* the package.

- You've *assessed it in terms of your goals, values and ideals, and in terms of your financial needs.*

- You've *researched the salaries of similar jobs* in this market.

- You've *considered how* you will negotiate.

Now, your options are:

1. You can accept:

   Thank you, I'd be delighted to accept your offer. When shall I schedule orientation?

2. You can decline:

   Thank you for the offer. I've decided to take a position which directly correlates with my degree. I've enjoyed talking with all of you and look forward to a cordial business relationship.

3. You can negotiate. This conversation is known as **the $1000 five minute phone call**.

   You call the supervisor who made the offer and say: *I'm very enthusiastic about the position and the goals of your organization. I've reassessed my financial situation and have found with student loans and moving costs, I really need to make $_____.*

   Can anything be done to increase the offer?
   (This last sentence is key — don't forget it!)

Notice that you *have not made demands*, but have politely suggested that you need a living wage, given the standard of living in that particular city and given the market rate for the job at hand.

The company will do *one* of the following things:

1. The *offer cannot be increased,* but the company hopes you will accept anyway because it is a good opportunity for you.

2. The *salary cannot be increased, but the compensation package can be altered*—for instance, a review at 6 months for a possible raise rather than at a year, or increase in co-payment for insurance or earlier vesting in a 401 K.

3. The *organization is willing to increase* the salary to $_____.

Of course, your fear is that the company will withdraw the offer. Remember, the ball is in your court. However, what if the worst case scenario does happen?

- If the offer is withdrawn, is this a place where you'd want to work, where you were pressured to making commitments on little information and without time to consider options?

- Wouldn't you begin to wonder what was *wrong* with the package?

When is it **NOT** a good idea to negotiate?

- When you have *already stated* that a specific salary range is reasonable. You can't increase the range *in hindsight.*

- If the employment application asks what you are making now, so as to just top it, fill that blank in like this: you're looking for compensation that coincides with your training and experience. *Don't elaborate.*

If you've been through several series of interviews and no offer is forthcoming, take yourself in your corporation's hands and *call your last interviewer to ask* what can be done to improve my:

- interview skills,
- portfolio,
- appearance,
- attitude, and
- posture to heighten the probability of an offer for a position?

You may be surprised by the answer. Do it. An alternative is to work with the employment counselor or career advisor at your school or university, and role-play some interviews with the career advisor to improve your skills. What you'll learn will help you to make the *right future choices* in support of your corporation.

A final word:

- Your attitude is in your complete control.

- ***Have fun!* Approach each interview looking forward to meeting fascinating people.**

- ***Thank them*** for the opportunity to meet and discuss your dynamic field.

*Resource consulted: John L. LaFevre, *How You Really Get Hired*. See Resource List included in the Addenda of this book.

Figuring out *how much is enough* to negotiate for:

We've done some financial planning, so that you know *how much you need per month* (expenses and savings plan). (See the section on Financial Management on page 33.) You've multiplied your Monthly Needs by 12 so that you know *how much you need per year.* (You do, don't you?) How do you get from *what you need* (net) to *what you'll actually have to be paid* (gross) to *take home what you need (…net!)*?

From your Financial Management Section:

1. figure out your monthly needs (Expenses and Savings Plan) _____

2. multiply your monthly net figure by 12 months to arrive at your yearly net
   _____ x 12 = _____ = yearly *net* (*take-home*)

3. figure out your federal tax bracket
   a. (hypothetically, for our purposes: 17%) _____
   b. (in states with income tax, the state income tax must be added as well)
      _____

4. your Social Security contribution
   a. *if employed by others* is 7.84%
   b. your Social Security contribution *if employed by yourself* (freelance) is 15.68%,
      - 7.84% *as an employee, and*
      - another 7.84% as *an employer*

5. add your taxes + your Social Security contribution

   a. employed by others: 7.84% + 17% = 24.84 % or
   b. self-employed: 15.68% + 17% = 32.68%

6. take 24.84% or 32.68% from 100% to obtain your *complement*
   100% − 24.84%= 75.16% (employed by others)
   100% − 32.68% = 67.32% (self-employed)

   and change the % to a decimal:
   a. 75.16% = .7516 or
   b. 67.32% = .6732

7. to get *from* your *net* (take-home) *to* your *gross* salary, **Divide your net** **by the complement.**

What if this is an *unrealistic* starting salary? You have a few options:

- cut your needs (sell your car, take on a roommate)
- cut down on entertainment expenses, phone calls, etc.
- take on a second job
- freelance work

Be realistic about your options and make a plan.

You're offered a salary?

How do you know if the take-home pay (net) from this salary (gross) is enough to meet your expenses and savings plan (net)?

- to get from a salary offered (gross) to the net (take home pay) to see if it covers your needs and obligations,

- **multiply** the gross salary *by the complement.*

Example

To get from gross to net, **multiply** by the complement of taxes and Social Security.

- I'm offered $24,000 per year to be employed by a company.

- How can I figure how much take-home pay that will be?

  1. add taxes and Social Security together.
  2. subtract the total from 100% to arrive at the complement.
  3. change the percent to a decimal.
  4. multiply $24,000 by the result of #3 above.

- $24,000 x [100 % − (7.84% + 17%)] = $18,038.40

In this example, federal income tax is assumed to be 17%, 0% state income tax. R*emember*, the more you earn, the more you pay in federal and state income taxes, but *Social Security remains constant.*

How do you know how much salary to negotiate for?

- to get from your net (which you figured out in the Financial Management section on page 34), take your net and

- **divide** by the complement of tax and Social Security contribution.

Example

To get from net (take-home) to gross salary, **divide** by the complement of taxes and Social Security.

- My monthly bills are $1,500 and my financial plans require $500 per month, for a total monthly net of $2,000.

- My yearly net would then be $2,000 x 12 months.

- $2,000 x 12 = $24,000 net salary required.

- How can I figure out what salary would result in a take-home (net) of $24,000?

  1. add taxes and Social Security together.
  2. subtract the total from 100% to arrive at the complement.
  3. change the percent to a decimal.
  4. divide $24,000 by the result of #3.

- $24,000 \div [100 - (7.84\% + 22\%)] = \$ 34,207.53$.

In this example, the federal income tax is assumed to be 22%, 0% state income tax.

What if you are a freelance designer or illustrator?

Example

You are offered $2,000 for a job. How much do you get to keep? How much should you set aside for taxes and Social Security?

1. add your taxes and Social Security together.
2. take them away from 100%.
3. change the % into a decimal.
4. **multiply** by the tax and Social Security complement to arrive at your net for the job.

- $2000 x [100% − (7.84% + 7.84% + 17%)] = $1,346.40

- $653.60 is your tax and Social Security contribution.

  Tip for the self-employed: Don't forget to set up an account to save taxes and Social Security. They will come due, whether you have the money saved or not! Wouldn't you feel silly having to borrow from the bank to pay taxes?

In this example, federal income tax is assumed to be 17%, 0% state income tax.

What if the **dealer, agent, broker, or sales representative** you have hired to sell your work takes 18% of the contract fee (fees are negotiable)?

Example

You are offered $2,000 for a job, and your sales rep takes 18%. How can I figure out what my take-home pay is?

1. You take 18% from 100% to determine how much you have left and how much you have to pay taxes on.

   - 100% −18% = 82%
   - $2,000 x .82 = $1,640
   - Who pays taxes on the $360 difference? Your sales rep!

2. Now proceed as in the previous example.

   - $1640 x [100% − (7.84% + 7.84% = 17%)] = $1104.05 (net pay)

Tip for the self-employed: create a savings account for your taxes and Social Security. Not only will you earn interest, you will not be tempted to spend the money that is owed to the IRS and Social Security.

In this example, federal income tax is assumed to be 17%, 0% state income tax.

What if you're offered a full-time job at $12.00 per hour in wages? Can you afford to take this job?

Example

1. Multiply the number of hours in a typical work week (40) by the number of weeks per year (52).
   - 40 x 52 = 2,080 hours per year

2. Multiply the $12 per hour by the hours in a typical year.
   - 2,080 x $12 = $24,960 *gross yearly* wages

3. What is the take-home pay on a $12 per hour job?

   - add taxes and Social Security.
   - take them away from 100%.
   - change the % to a decimal.
   - multiply by the complement to arrive at net.

   - $24,960 x [100 − (7.84% + 17%)] = $18,759.94 *take-home (net)* wages.

If your monthly bills and financial plan require $2,000 per month in take-home pay ($24,000 per year net), then you *cannot* afford this job. However, if your monthly bills and financial plan require $1,500 per month in take-home pay ($18,000 per year net), then you *can* take the job.

In this example, federal income tax is assumed to be 17%, 0% state income tax.

What if you are working on contract? What is your take-home pay?

Example

Your contract pays you $40 per hour and is arranged for by an agency which takes 10% of your yearly salary for placing you. It is made clear that you are an independent contractor and will pay your own taxes and Social Security.

- *First*, pay your contractor (agency).
  1. Figure out your gross pay per year: multiply the number of hours in a work week by the number of weeks in a year.

     40 x 52 = 2,080 hours per year

  2. Figure out your gross wages per year.

     2,080 x $40 = $83,200

  3. Figure the complement: 100% – 10% = 90%

  4. Change the 90% to .9

  5. Multiply by the complement.

     .9 x $83,200 = $74,880

     This is the gross pay you'll figure your take-home (net) on.

  6. The $83,2000 – $74,880 = $8,320 is the 10% fee that belongs to your agency. Figure your take-home based on $74,880.

Could you multiply $83,200 by 10% and take that from $83,200? Sure. Either way works.

- *Next*, figure your net net.

  1. add taxes and Social Security.
  2. subtract from 100%.
  3. change the % to a decimal.
  4. multiply by the complement to arrive at net net.

  $74,880 x [100% − (7.84% + 7.84% + 28%) = $42,172.25 net net

  What happens to the $30,423? Taxes and Social Security! Remember your savings account for that purpose? Aren't you glad you didn't spend the whole $83,200?

In this example, federal income tax is assumed to be 28%, 0% state income tax.

Tip: It is clear that if you work on contract, you need to be a good money manager. Some people who work on contract or freelance book themselves as tightly as possible, but when a break comes, they work temporary jobs so as not to have to dip into their savings accounts.

You're moving to Chicago

You want to have a lifestyle comparable to the one you have in Seattle. How much will you have to make (gross) to take-home (net) enough to live as well as you have in Seattle?

You can figure this out if you know 2 things:
1. your net in Seattle
2. the relative cost of living in Chicago

Example

You know you need $1,500 per month in take-home pay to live well in Seattle (or $1,500 x 12 = $18,000 per year take-home or net salary).

You know the standard of living is 30% higher in Chicago. How do you find this out? Get a newspaper from Chicago and compare one bedroom apartments or loaves of bread in each city. For instance, a one-bedroom apartment in Seattle might be $1,000 while a similar one in Chicago might be $1, 334.

- 1,000 ÷ 1,334 = .75 or 75%
- 100% − 75% = 25%
- Therefore, the standard of living in Chicago is +25% compared to Seattle.
- **or** go to virtualmove.com, which will figure this for you.

Using Seattle's standard of living as **base** or 100%, Chicago's standard of living is 125%.

- $1,500 x 1.25 = $1,875 take-home (net) per month.
- $1,875 x 12 = $22,500 take-home (net) per year needed in Chicago.

How do I figure out what gross salary I'd need to cover $22,500 net?

1. add taxes and Social Security.
2. take them away from 100% to arrive at the complement.
3. convert a % to a decimal.
4. **divide** by the complement to arrive at gross.

- [$1,500 x 1.25 x 12] ÷ [100 − (7.84 + 22)] = $32,069.56

Remember, the more you earn, the more you pay in income taxes, but Social Security remains constant.

Note: all income tax figures are for states *without* income tax *except where noted*. For states **with** *income tax*, **add** the *state income tax* percentage to the *federal income tax* percentage *and Social Security* contribution, and subtract from 100% as usual.

The Social Security contribution remains constant unless amended by Congress, while the federal and state income taxes **slide**, depending on income, up to a certain maximum, keyed on the latest tax legislation.

These broad calculations should in no way replace a competent certified public accountant, and are intended only to give some guidance to salary calculations and negotiation.

Now, put what you know into practice. *Complete the following worksheet* to practice what you know about crunching numbers.

Wage/ Math Tips

1. **Complement:** tax and Social Security multiplier (add federal income tax, state income tax and Social Security contribution together, subtract from 100% [or 1.00] to arrive at complement)

2. **Net to Gross** (small to large): **divide** by complement

3. **Gross to Net** (large to small): **multiply** by complement

4. **Hourly wage**: multiply by 2080 (hr/yr) to arrive at gross yearly wages

Cut out Wage/Math Tips and put it in your wallet so you can have it handy for power negotiations!

1. You're offered a salary by a company of $28,000 per year.

  - How much will you take home (net)?
  - Assume a 17% federal tax bracket and no state income tax. (Ahem. Social Security?)
  - Show your math.

2. You need $1,500 per month to meet your needs.

  - That's $_____ per year.
  - What salary will you need to cover that?
  - Assume a 17% federal tax bracket and no state income tax. (Ahem! Social Security?)
  - Show your math.

3. You're offered $6,000 for a freelance job attained by an agent or artist's representative.

  - He'll take 15%.
  - Assume a 17% federal tax bracket and no state income tax.
  - Here's what's left after you've paid your rep and *before* taxes and Social Security deposit: _____
  - Remember, free lancers are self-employed (employee **and** employer's Social Security).

  - Your net (take home) is? _____
  - Show your math.

4. You're offered a full-time job for $15.00 per hour.

  - How much is that per year? _____

  - If your obligations and needs are about $18,000 year ($1,500 per month), will you be able to cover your bills with a $15 per hour job? (Assume a 20% federal tax bracket and no state income tax.) _____

5. You're working *on contract* for $35 per hour. Your agency, which set up the deal, takes out its 10% fee.

  - Assume no state income tax.
  - Assume a 25% federal income tax rate. (Ahem! You are responsible for both the employee's and employer's Social Security contribution.)
  - What is your net (take-home) pay for the year?
  - Use complements and show your math.

  Gross pay _____
  After contract fee is taken out _____
  Net Net (after taxes, Social Security are withheld) _____

6. You're moving to Los Angeles to take a job. In Seattle your expenses are around $1,200 per month, or $14,400 per year. LA has a standard of living which is about 30% higher than Seattle's.

  - How would you figure out what kind of salary you'll need to live a comparable lifestyle?
  - Assume a federal tax bracket of 20% and a California state income tax of 8%. (Ahem! Social Security?)
    Complement? _____

  _____ *net* in LA
  _____ *gross* in LA

YEA! Good for you! A job in a field you love! It looks like all the hard work paid off.

Your *next step* is to phone your contact at the company and discuss your compensation package. You can do this. *If you can come to an agreement which both of you think is fair*, then you can accept!

Giving notice

- It is important to give your present employer *at least* 2 weeks notice to find a replacement worker when you resign your position.

- Be aware that you may be asked to leave immediately upon giving notice, so a savings plan works very well here! You may even be escorted from the building or given ½ hour to clean out your desk—with supervision! If you are working on information that the company considers vital, you will probably find your departure somewhat abrupt. Prepare yourself.

- Your new employer will respect your need to be honorable, as s/he will want the same from you in the event that you leave your new place of employment. Your new employer might ask you to work immediately and put a bit of pressure on you to do so, but you'll of course mention that s/he would want the same courtesy.

Man is asked to make of himself what he is supposed to become to fulfill his destiny. —Paul Tillich

Remember, you will not want to create an enemy, but leave on a cordial note so that you may do business together again.

You can offer to work on the week-end or transition during your free time to ease the burden on the new company. Often, a company will not start the interview process until it is really desperate for a new worker. Your new employer may fuss about the fact that you cannot start immediately, but you really will want to make a good segue from one job to the other.

It will be in the best long term interests of your own corporation if you make this a smooth transition, honoring the needs of both your new employer and your old employer.

Finally, **thank everyone** who has been instrumental in your job hunt. **Inform** *everyone* you've interviewed with about your new opportunity, and tell them you're looking forward to doing business with them.

- You might say:

  I've taken a position at XYZ Company as an ink and painter. Thank you for the time you gave me during the interviewing process. I enjoyed meeting you and look forward to a cordial business relationship.

You'll want to maintain your corporation's network. It's key to also keep in mind that the business community is small and that information about "bad actors" gets around...and so does praise for "stars." If you are cordial, professional, and demonstrate your talent and preparation, this information gets around too. *What goes around, comes around.* You can bet on it. Make sure what *goes around* about you is positive.

VI. Addenda

A, B, C

- **ancillary businesses**: those which support the main industry: like fabric design is to the fashion industry, or textile design is to fashion design or interior design

- **budget**: a financial plan, compared to actual expenses to assist in future planning

- **compensation package:** combination of salary, paid vacation, paid insurance (health, life, dental, vision), maternity and elder care leaves, child care, paid sick days, health club fees, parking and passes, among others

- **computer hardware:** computer equipment: processor, monitor, printer, cables, etc.

- **computer software:** programs which produce documents, edit film, recreate sound, etc.

The worst part of success is trying to find someone who is happy for you. —Bette Midler

D, E, F, G

- **demographics:** data on people organized by categories, such as profession, income, neighborhood, buying patters, etc. The collection of this data is particularly prevalent on the Internet.

- **downsizing:** see right sizing

- **dpi:** dots per inch (a measurement of screen display and printer resolution)

- **expenses:** *actual* expenditures (as opposed to a *budget* which is *planned* income and expenditures).

- **financial analysis:** comparison of the budget (plan) and actual income and expenses

- **401K:** pension plans in which the employer and employee both contribute pre-tax salary based on a published formula

- **GIF:** compressed file for line drawings and Internet images (an acronym for Graphics Interchange Format)

- **gig:** a show, an opportunity to perform

- **graphics:** a field which designs and produces print materials, the design of lettering and titles

H, I, J, K

- **hard returns:** hitting "Enter" or "Return" on your keyboard

- **industrial design:** design of product: furniture, communication hardware, lifestyle accessories, transportation devices

- **IPO:** initial public offering—many companies make up for mediocre salaries with stock options in the company. When the company goes public, those options hypothetically increase dramatically in value.

- **jpeg:** condensed color imaging files (an acronym for the people who wrote the standard for compressed color images—Joint Photographic Experts Group)

L, M, N

- **marketplace:** where buyers and sellers of goods and services meet

- **multi-media:** combination of many artistic endeavors; still and moving picture with sound and graphics

- **networking:** meeting and talking to people who become your network of associates

- **new media:** media that exists in the digital domain (Website design, on-line magazines, video games, etc.)

O, P, Q

- **open ended questions:** questions which open a conversation; cannot be answered in one word

- **popular press:** periodicals which can be purchased at the grocery store: *Rolling Stone, Inc., Cinefex*

- **post production:** addition of graphics, editing of video, music, film after the performance

- **ppi:** pixels per inch (screen resolution)

- **professional organization:** group of like-minded professionals that meets regularly to support its industry: AIA, IDSA, AIGA, GAG, FGI, SIGGRAPH, IICS, etc.

R, S, T

- **reorganization:** see right sizing

- **right–sizing:** industry buzzword for eliminating job categories to reduce waste; usually a short term strategy since abrupt change undermines morale. Especially prevalent in mergers and acquisitions.

- **salary:** based on a yearly figure, independent of hours worked, usually no overtime paid

- **shake out:** survival of the fittest in each category of business

- **SIGS:** special interest groups

- **trade, the:** refers to the business community as opposed to the general public

- **trade journals:** periodicals that are directed toward one type of business, such as the fashion industry, design, advertising, graphic design, among many others. *WWD, ID, Adweek, HOW, Architecture,* etc.

- **trends in the marketplace:** changes in business in general categories over 2 – 3 years or longer.

U, V, W, X, Y, Z

- **venture capital:** money invested in new, and therefore risky, businesses

- **wages:** amount of money paid for hourly work, overtime compensated

1. You're offered a salary by a company of $28,000 per year.
   - How much will you take home (net)?
   - Assume a 17% federal tax bracket and no state income tax. (Ahem. Social Security?)
   - Show your math.

$28,000 x [100% − (17% + 7.84%)] = $28,000 x .7516 = $21,044.80

2. You need $1,500 per month to meet your needs.
   - That's $ __18,000__ per year.
   - What salary will you need to cover that?
   - Assume a 17% federal tax bracket and no state income tax. (Ahem! Social Security?)
   - Show your math.

$18,000 ÷ [100% − (17% + 7.84%)] = $18,000 ÷ .7516 = $23,948.91

3. You're offered $6,000 for a freelance job attained by an agent or artist's representative.
   - The artist's rep's fee will be 15%.
   - Assume a 17% Federal tax bracket and no state income tax.
   - Here's what's left after you've paid your rep and *before* taxes and Social Security deposit: **$6,000 x (100% − 15%) = $6,000 x .85 = $5,100**
     - *$900 goes to the rep who pays tax on that income*
   - Remember, free lancers are self-employed (employee **and** employer's Social Security). **15.68%**
   - Your net (take home) is?
   - Show your math.

$5,100 x [100% − (17% + 15.68%)] = 5,100 x .6732 = $3,433.32

4. You're offered a full-time job for $15.00 per hour.

- How much is that per year?

   52 weeks/year x 40 hours/week = 2,080 hours/year
   2,080/hours per year x $15/hour = $31,200 gross wages

- If your obligations and needs are about $18,000 year ($1,500 per month), will you be able to cover your bills with a $15 per hour job? (Assume a 20% federal tax bracket and no state income tax.)

   $31,200 x [100% − (20% + 7.84%)] = $31,200 x .7216 = $22,233.12

- **Yes, you'd be able to take the job and have a little extra for a vacation, too.**

5. You're working *on contract* for $35 per hour. Your agency, which set up the deal, takes out its 10% fee.
   - Assume no state income tax.
   - Assume a 25% federal income tax rate. (Ahem! You are responsible for both the employ**ee**'s and employ**er**'s Social Security contribution.)
   - What is your net (take-home) pay for the year?
   - Use complements and show your math.

   Gross pay

   $35/hour x 2,080 hours/year = $72,800 *(yippee!)*

   After contract fee is taken out

   $72,800 x (100% − 10%) = $72,800 x .9 = $65,520 *(still pretty good)*

   Net net (after taxes, Social Security) _____

   $65,520 x [100% − (25% + 15.68%)] = $65,520 x .5932 = $38,866.46

6. You're moving to Los Angeles to take a job. In Seattle your expenses are around $1,200 per month, or $14,400 per year.

- LA has a standard of living which is about 30% higher than Seattle's.

    - **Use the standard of living in Seattle as base (or 100%) and add 30% to the base for 130% or 1.3**

- How would you figure out what kind of salary you'll need to live a comparable lifestyle?
- Assume a federal tax bracket of 20% and a California state income tax of 8%. (Ahem! Social Security?)

- Complement? **100% – (20% + 7.84%) = 72.15% = .7216**

    A. **$14,400 x 130% = $14,400 x 1.3 = $18,720 *net salary* in LA**

    B. **$18,720 ÷ [100% – (20% + 8% + 7.84%) =**
       $18,720 ÷ .6416 = $29,177.06 *gross* salary in LA

    A. Want to know what the comparable gross salary would need to be in Seattle?

       $14,400 ÷ [100% – (20% + 7.84% (no state tax in WA)] =
       $14,400 ÷ .7216 = $19,956.65 gross salary in Seattle

```
┌ ─ ─ ─ ─ ─ ─ ─ ─ ─ ─ ─ ─ ─ ─ ─ ┐
    Resources for Leads I and II
└ ─ ─ ─ ─ ─ ─ ─ ─ ─ ─ ─ ─ ─ ─ ─ ┘
```

Help! Where do you find the resources for Leads?

Your city's Public Library: *Business Department*

- **Ask** the business librarian for help to find the reference you need—that's his/her job.

- Your local library often has CD-ROMs on demographics (statistics on age, profession, types of companies, income level of residents, etc.) of all types.

- Books of lists are published yearly, often by periodical companies, and are an especially rich resource.

Books for creative disciplines

Northwest Area

- *Book of Lists* published by <u>Puget Sound Business Journal</u>)—all creative disciplines
- *Media, Inc. Book of Lists* (lists top design firms, ad agencies, artists reps, etc. for multi-media, illustration, graphic design, advertising, radio and TV, etc.)
- *Media Index*
- *Northwest Creative Index* (yellow pages of self-promo)

Nationwide

- *American Showcase* (art/photo related companies)
- *Audiovideo Marketplace* (4,000 businesses providing audiovisual services + details)
- *Creative Black Book* (art/photo related companies)
- *Editor and Publisher's Yearbook* (lists all US newspapers)
- *Gale Directory of Publications and Broadcast Media*
- *Hollywood Reporter Blue Book* (all movie-related resources, including special effects and costuming, set and stage design, animation houses)
- *International Radio, TV, Broadcast & Programming*
- *Locations* (official directory of Association of Film Commissioners International)
- *Radio & TV Career Directory*

- *Recording Industry Sourcebook*
- *Sheldon's Retail Guides* (list major retailers + details)
- *Standard Directory of Advertising Agencies* (Red Book) (lists ad agencies + details)
- *Standard Rate and Data Service* (national listing of magazines + details)
- *Telephone Yellow Pages* (entire US on CD-Rom)
- *Television and Cable Factbook* (national index of TV stations, cable and suppliers to industry)
- *The Big Green Book* (NW music industry directory)
- *The Index (*PNW film, video, TV, audio production index, published by Media, Inc.)
- *The Yellow Pages of Rock* (AV Marketplace) (list audio, AV, computer systems, film, video programming companies + details)

Traditional books for lists *of a general business nature*

(International students should check international trade directories and those companies who do business overseas.)

Northwest
- *Contacts Influential* (lists area employers)
- *King County Manufacturers Guide* (lists by product + details)
- *Washington Register* (4,500 firms + details)

Nationwide
- *Directory of American Firms Operating in Foreign Countries*
- *Directory of Foreign Firms Operating in the United States* (lists, details, and US affiliates)
- *Dun & Bradstreet Directory* (mid to large firms in sales + details)
- *International Trade Directory* (state firms engaged in exporting and importing, goods and services + details)
- *Moody's Register Manual* (publicly held companies + details, arranged in interest groups)
- *National Directory of State Agencies* (contact person in each of 102 functions in each state + details)

- *Plant and Product Directory* (top 1,000 industrial corporations and details)
- *Principal International Businesses—The World Marketing Directory* (55,000 major companies operating in 133 nations + details)
- *Standard & Poors Corporation Records* (similar to Moody's, arranged alphabetically)
- *Thomas Register* (listing of US manufacturing companies)

Trade Journals are full of up-to-date printed information.

- Their turn-around time is about *4 months* (as opposed to 10 months or more for book publication).

- They include profiled artists/designers are accompanied by addresses, phone, e-mail addresses on the back 3 pages of the publication.

- **Use these for Leads I and II.**

- Most publish **yearly directories** *of talent and resources.* Look for a resource list in *How, CA, ID*, among many others.

- Some publications are found in the stacks, some in reserve. ***Ask your librarian!***

Adobe	*Aperture*
Advertising Age	*Aramco World*
Adweek	*Arbitare*
Agent & Manager	*Arcade*
Airbrush Action	*Architectural Digest*
American Artist	*Architectural Record*
American Cinematographer	*Archive*
American Music Newsletter	*Art Direction*
American Photo	*ASMP Bulletin*
Animation Journal	

Before & After   Broadcasting & Cable
Billboard

Car Styling   Communication Arts (CA)
CD-ROM Professional   Computer Artist
CD-ROM Today   Computer Graphics World
Cinefex   Conde Nast Traveler
CMYK   Contemporary Christian Music
Comics Journal   Country Fever
Commercial Image   Creation
Creative: the Magazine of Promotion and Marketing

Design News   Digital Video
Design World   Directives West
Desktop Publisher's Journal   DNR (Daily News Record)

Electronic Media   Electronic Publishing
EQ (Project recording and Sound Techniques)
Exhibit Builder

Film & Video Magazine

Graphis   Guitar Player

High Color   How

ID (International Design)   Interior Design
Interiors

Lighting Dimensions   Live Sound
Locations

Macuser
Macworld
Maximum Rock 'n Roll
MBI Music Business International
Metropolis
Microsoft
MIDI Magazine
Mix

Modern Plastics
MR (Men's Wear Retailing)
Multimedia World

Music & Sound Retailer
Music Connection

New Media

New Media Age

Option

PC Graphics & Video
Performance
Photo District News
Photo Electronic Imaging
Photo Pro
Photo Techniques
Pollstar

Popular Mechanics
Post
Print
Printer's Northwest Trader
Pro Sound News
Professional Photographer
Progressive Architecture

Rangefinder
Rappages
Recording

Rock & Rap Confidential
Rolling Stone

Spin
Sportswear International

Step-by-step Electronic Design
Stores

TCI (Theater Crafts International)
Technique
Television Broadcast
Tobe

Travel & Leisure
Travel Industry Newsletter
TV Technology

Vibe
Video Systems
Videography
VM+SD (Visual Merchandising and Store Design)

Videomaker
View Camera

W
Wired

Woodsmith
WWD (Women's Wear Daily)

Popular Press includes those publications found on the news stand, in supermarkets, and at bookstores. *Check sections of periodicals for business trends, changing markets, opportunities, and opening market niches.* This category includes

- *Spin*
- *Wired*
- *Inc.*
- *Newsweek, Time, Business Week*
- *Vogue*
- *GQ*
- *Vanity Fair*
- *Local newspapers*
- *International newspapers*
- *And a plethora of others, including Websites for print publications.*

Websites and job search engines are an increasingly rich area for job search. New sites and links appear (and disappear) daily.

The Monster Board: http://www.monster.com has become dominant in the last few years. Others:

- America's Job Bank: http://www.ajb.dni.us
- CareerMosaic**:** http://www.careermosaic.com
- The Main Quad: http://develop.mainquad.com
- Online Career Center: http://www.occ.com
- Yahoo! Classifieds: http://classifieds.yahoo.com
- Classifieds of 6 major newspapers (*Boston Globe, Chicago Tribune, LA Times, NY Times, San Jose Mercury News and Washington Post):* http://www.careerpath.com
- Online Career Center: http://www.occ.com/occ
- JobSmart: http://www.JobSmart salary surveys
- Graphic Designers: http://www.Artifexnet.comm

Additional material for job search, career choice, personality assessment, and financial management:

- There are many excellent works published on various parts of job search in general and non-creative professional practice.

- Check the *Resource List* section in the Addenda for specific references.

National and International Art and Design Oriented Professional Associations

Organization	Initials	www
American Advertising Federation	AAF	www.aaf.org
American Advertising Federation (AD 2 for twentysomethings)	Ad2	www.ad2.org
American Architectural Manufacturers Association	AAMA	www.aamanet.org
American Association of Advertising Agencies	AAAA	www.aaaa.org
American Center for Design	ACD	www.ac4d.org
American Furniture Manufacturers Association	AFMA	www.afmahp.org
American Institute of Architects	AIA	www.aia.org
American Institute of Graphic Arts	AIGA	www.aiga.org
American Marketing Association	AMA	www.ama.org
American Society of Furniture Designers	ASFD	www.arcat.com
American Society of Interior Designers	ASID	www.asid.org
American Society of Media Photographers	ASMP	www.asmp.org
American Textile Manufacturers Institute	ATMI	www.atmi.org
Architectural League of New York		www.archleague.org
Art Directors Club (ADC+ first initial of city or state)	ADC	www.adcny.org
Asian American Architects & Engineers Association	AAAEA	www.aaaea.org
Associated Landscape Contractors of America	ALCA	www.alca.org
Association for Suppliers of Printing & Publishing Technologies	NPES	www.npes.org
Association of Computing Machinery	ACM	www.acm.org
Association of Graphic Communications	AGC	www.agcomm.org
Association of Independent Commercial Producers	AICP	www.aicp.com
Association of Professional Design Firms	APDF	www.apaf.org
Association of Professional Model Makers	APMM	www.modelmakers.org
Association Typografique International	ATYPI	www.atypi.org
Association for Women in Computing	AWC	www.awc-hq.org
Audio Engineering Society	AES	www.aes.org

Broadcast Designers' Association International	BDA	www.bdaweb.com
Business and Institutional Furniture Manufacturers' Association	BIFMA	www.fma.com
Business Products Industry Association	BPIA	www.bpia.org
Color Association of the United States		www.colorassociation.com
Color Marketing Group	CMG	www.colormarketing.org
Corporate Design Foundation	CDF	www.cdf.org
Creative Arts Guild	CAG	www.creativeartsguild.org
Design Management Institute	DMI	www.dmi.org
Digital Media Alliance	DMA	www.digitalmedia.net
Fashion Group International	FGI	www.fgi.org
Graphic Artists Guild	GAG	www.gag.org
Human Factors & Ergonomics Society	HFES	www.hfes.org
Illuminating Engineering Society of North America	IESNA	www.iesna.org
Industrial Designers Society of America	IDSA	www.idsa.org
Institute of Packaging Professionals	IOPP	www.pkgmatters.com
Institute of Store Planners	ISP	www.ispo.org
Interactive Services Association	ISA	www.isa/net/isa
International Association of Amusement Parks and Attractions	IAAPA	www.iaapa.org
International Association of Lighting Designers	IALD	www.iald.org
International Digital Imaging Association	IDIA	www.idea.org
International Furnishings & Design Association	IDFA	www.idfa.com
International Interactive International Communications Society	IICS	www.iics.org
International Interior Design Association	IIDA	www.iida.org
International Television Association	ITVA	www.itva.org
Musicians Network		www.MusiciansNetwork.com
National Academy of Recording Arts & Sciences	NARAS	www.grammy.com
National Academy of TV Arts & Sciences	NATAS	www.emmyonline.org
National Cartoonists Society	NCS	www.reuben.org
National Society of Visual Merchandisers	NACM	www.visualmerch.org

Organization of Black Designers	OBD	www.core77.com
Society for Environmental Graphic Design	SEGD	www.segd.org
Society of Broadcast Engineers	SBE	www.sbe.org
Society of Motional Picture & Television Engineers	SMPTE	www.smpte.org
Society of Publication Designers	SPD	www.spd.org
Society of the Plastics Industry	SPI	www.soplas.org
Software Information Industry Association	SIIA	www.siia.org
Special Interest Group on Computer Graphics	SIGGRAPH	www.siggraph.org
Trade Show Exhibitors Association	TSEA	www.tsea.org
United States Institute of Theater Technology, Inc.	USITT	www.usitt.org
Western Art Directors Club	WADC	www.wadc.org
Women in Communications	WICI	www.wici.org
Women in Film	WIF	www.wif.org

```
Resource List:  Books consulted in researching this book
```

Anderson, Nancy	*Work with Passion*	New York, NY	Carroll & Graff	1989
Beatty, Richard	*The Perfect Cover Letter*	New York, NY	Wiley	1989
Berryman, Gregg	*Designing Creative Résumés*	Menlo Park, CA	Crisp Publications	1990
Boldt, Lawrence	*Zen & The Art of Making a Living*	New York NY	Arkana	1993
Bolles, Richard N.	*The Three Boxes of Life*	Berkeley, CA	Ten Speed Press	1981
	What Color is Your Parachute?	Berkeley, CA	Ten Speed Press	1989
Burd, Rachel (ed.)	*Graphic Artists Guild Handbook*	New York , NY	G.A.G./Northlight	1994
Cameron & Bryan	*The Artist's Way*	Los Angeles, CA	Tarcher/Perigee	1992
Caplin, Lee (ed.)	*The Business of Art*	Englewood Cliffs, NJ	Prentice Hall	1989
Carlson, Linda	*989 Great Part-Time Jobs in Seattle*	Seattle, WA	Barrett St. Productions	1995+
	How to Find a Good Job in Seattle	Seattle, WA	Barrett St. Productions	1997+
Deep & Sussman	*Smart Moves*	Reading, MA	Addison-Wesley	1990
	Yes, You Can!	Reading, MA	Perseus Books	1996
Farr, J. Michael	*The Very Quick Job Search*	Indianapolis, IN	JIST Works,	1991
Fisher, Helen	*American Salaries & Wage Survey*	Detroit, MI	Gale Research	1995
Fleishman, Michael	*Getting Started as a Freelance Illustrator or Designer*	Cincinnati, OH	North Light	1990
Francis, Dave	*Effective Problem Solving*	London, England	Routledge	1990
Hacker, Diana	*The Bedford Handbook for Writers*	Boston, MA	St.Martin's Press	1994
Haubenstock & Joselit	*Career Opportunities in Art*	New York, NY	Facts on File	1994
Ito, Dee	*Careers in the Visual Arts*	New York, NY	Watson-Guptil	1993
Kennedy, J.L.	*Job Interviews for Dummies*	Foster City, CA	IDG Books	1996
	Résumés for Dummies	Foster City, CA	IDG Books	1996
Keirsey & Bates	*Please Understand Me*	DelMar, CA	Prometheus Nemesis	1984
Koberg & Bagnall	*The Universal Traveler*	Los Altos, CA	Crisp Publications	1991

LaFevre, John L.	*How You Really Get Hired*	New York, NY	Prentice Hall	1986
Lauer, David A.	*Design Basics*	New York, NY	HBJ	1990
McNally, David	*Even Eagles Need a Push*	New York, NY	Dell Publishing	1994
Malloy, John T.	*John T. Malloy's New Dress for Success*	New York, NY	Warner Books	1988
Repa, Barbara K.	*Your Rights in the Workplace*	Berkeley, CA	Nolo Press	1996
Ryan, Robin	*60 Seconds and You're Hired*	Manassas Park, VA	Impact Publications	1994
Sher, Barbara	*I Could Do Anything…*	New York, NY	Delacorte Press	1994
Simon et al.	*Values Clarification: A Handbook of Practical Strategies*	New York, NY	Hart Publishing	1972
Sourcebook Editor	*ID Magazine*	New York, NY	ID Magazine	1996+
Stoodley, Martha	*Information Interviewing*	Chicago, IL	Ferguson Publications	1996
Tieger & Barron-Tieger	*Do What You Are*	Boston, MA	Little, Brown	1995
Wallach, Janet	*Looks that Work*	New York, NY	Viking Press	1986
Weinberg, Janice	*How to Win the Job You Really Want*	New York, NY	Henry Holt	1989
Yates, Martin J.	*Knock 'Em Dead*	Avon, MA	Adams Media	1998+

*Note: + after the year indicates annual or biennial updates

Index

U, V, W, X, Y, Z